HONOUR, HEELS *and* HEADSCARVES

Real-Life stories of Women from Istanbul

ISBN: 8461660587
ISBN 13: 978-8461660582
Translation into English: Rebekah Jane Rhodes

Cover design: Pete Garceau
Photograph: Zeynep Gün
ISBN: 978-84-616-6058-2

Second Edition: May2013. *Honour, Heels and Headscarves.* Create Space

July, 2013 *Honour, Heels and Headscarves.* Digital Editions

Second edition: April 2012. *En el Harén de Estambul* (digital version). Digital editions (epub and mobi formats) produced by Booknook.biz.

First edition: June 2009. *En el Harén de Estambul.* Styria de Ediciones y Publicaciones S.L.

HONOUR, HEELS *and* HEADSCARVES

Real-Life stories of Women from Istanbul

Translated by Rebekah Jane Rhodes

Carla De la Vega

For Salva

Contents

Preface

Let me introduce Zelal. After thirty-two years weighed down with suffering, life is now slipping from her grasp. “They want to kill me. I don’t want to die; there are so many things still to do. I haven’t done anything wrong. My only mistake was to have been honest—to have trusted, and been too naïve. I don’t want to die. I don’t want to, I don’t want to....Since I was born they’ve been killing me little by little. They didn’t let me go to university because it was for whores. And look what I’ve become...a prostitute. Am I really any different?”

I would like you to meet Sennur too. When I saw her for the first time she was twenty-three years old, devising ingenious ways to get into the university wearing an Islamic headscarf, despite this being banned under Turkish law. I can reveal from the outset that she has never kissed her boyfriend, although they have being going out together for over two years. “The Qur’an says: do not come close to sex because one thing can lead to another. This means that you can’t have sexual relations but also that you must avoid everything that comes before, all of those things that can incite you to do it. We shouldn’t touch each other or kiss. That’s why I don’t look at him. He crossed the line once and touched my hand. I liked it but it goes against my beliefs and made me feel bad. I’d like to look at him but it’s impossible. The Book doesn’t allow it.”

Quite different is the viewpoint of the Turkish girls with long, flowing hair, impeccable manicures, and the shortest of skirts, who elegantly swing their hips on the dance floors of Istanbul’s nightclubs. Ayse, twenty-six, is not wearing the skimpiest outfit, but I can disclose that she lost her virginity some time ago. “It’s absolutely necessary to have sex before getting married....You need to know who you’re with! Maybe you’ve been with someone for years and you don't want to sleep with him, or suddenly you meet someone who drives you crazy—you know, love at first sight, the real thing—and you sleep with him the first day."

Rashel is a Sephardic Jew in her sixties who, like the other women, lives in old Constantinople, now Istanbul. She will recount her difficult tale of survival using that ancient derivative of Spanish known as Ladino. "I'm delighted to have grown old. Men didn't let me live. All of them thought that I would sleep with them. These Turks are all the same! I don't want anything more to do with them; they've ruined my life. How could I accept being married to someone who locked me away? I was stupid."

While I gradually became acquainted with the political and social scene of a new destination—this time, a majority-Muslim country—I became more and more intrigued by these women who inhabit a Turkey in constant debate between East and West, tradition and modernity, religion and secularism.

From the outset, the so-called honour crimes caught my attention; the most macabre, vile, savage, and despicable treatment of a woman under the pretext of saving men's good names. I was brought to tears by the story of a young Kurdish girl, raped by a neighbour, tortured by a relative, and repudiated by her husband, whose own family were intent on killing her because the rape had resulted in pregnancy. I felt so helpless reading this account that I decided to investigate further. It was difficult to get in touch with anyone who had escaped the lethal weapon of tradition, as most victims are closely protected. In the end, I managed it, and you have already met the woman I found. Her name is Zelal.

How could I have imagined that in a country with a majority-Muslim population, the Islamic headscarf would be banned at universities? Well, in Turkey this is the case and the most surprising part is to witness the imaginative strategies young women use to skirt this legislation. I have met many women who wear a veil and suffer the consequences of living in a country that refuses to accept them with this square of fabric covering their hair. I have had long discussions with them about the guidelines set out in the Qur'an and the situation of women in the Muslim world. Without a doubt, the most interesting is Sennur, who opened up to me and shared her most intimate secrets. As you have already heard, she does not want to know anything about sex.

I also encountered women without Islamic headscarves, in dizzying heels and revealing necklines, young women who chatted with me about work, independence, men, shopping, and hairdressers. Ayse is one of them and not to be missed.

Like anyone else from Spain, I had heard about the Sephardic Jews who were expelled from my country; yet, I had no idea that in twenty-first century Muslim Turkey there were people who still spoke Ladino. I was so surprised that I set out to further research the women (descendants of the Spanish Jews) from this community, an arduous task, given the almost insurmountable security measures with which the Jewish population in old Constantinople protect themselves. It reached the point that a security guard at one place of worship even accused me of being a terrorist. He did not suggest that I was actually carrying a bomb but that I was a spy, forming a mental map of the building's layout to pass on to my accomplices later. I had to endure his disproportionately aggressive attitude and leave without seeing Ortaköy Synagogue. Yet there at my side, to help me access another synagogue, was Rashel. Spending time with this woman and getting to know her better was certainly worth the effort.

This book is a compendium of the real-life accounts that caught my attention from the outset. Listen to these women; they have so much to share about their lives, fears, frustrations, and dreams, and the ever-changing country in which they live. Read their stories because in this book, for once, it is their lives that take centre stage. I have given them a voice because through their biographies it is possible to gain a deeper understanding of these Turkish women who, at times, seem so far removed from us, while at others, reflect so closely our own sentiments that we have no difficulty whatsoever identifying with them.

It is not my aim to perpetuate stereotypes with these portraits; there are uncountable types of women in any country and Turkey is no different. Nor do I wish to fall into coarse generalisations. This book, then, should not be taken as a manual, but rather, an attempt at understanding a little better those women you may come across in the streets of Istanbul.

Part 1

The Unwanted

Women exist
Our silence, the way we sit
The way we bow our heads
The way we looked at life
Was expected of us, until today

Women exist, women are, women are everywhere

We were silent and we waited
Life went on, we watched it
But said "enough," in the end
We will never again remain silent

Women exist, women are, women are everywhere

Kadinlar Vardir song "Women Exist"
From the album *Güldünya Sarkilari*

I

The Escape

She has to leave. It is the only solution, her only way out. She must flee Turkey and do so as quickly as possible. Time is running out: they are going to kill her. Her husband will do it and if not, then her own family.

They have already discovered her whereabouts. She has just hung up the phone and this was the message from her sister: "They know you're in Istanbul. Be careful."

She has to take flight, to leave the country. Here, her life has no future; the only option is to face her own death. Salvation is in Europe. There, perhaps, she will be beyond the far-reaching tentacles of the Kurdish mafia, the clans, the tribe. There she will be safe, free to study, and able to find fulfilment. Once and for all, she will change this life that has brought nothing but suffering, beatings, and anguish. This same life now reeks of death; it languishes, slips away, and runs counter to its natural course.

The nightmare she must now overcome started with her first cry as a newborn baby. When they announced her arrival, silence reigned; she was a girl and that was no cause for celebration. In fact, Zelal's father had a mind to beat her mother yet again, this time for having the nerve to bring a girl into the world and, even worse, into his house. Since that day, thirty-two years have gone by.

Leaving Istanbul is the only alternative now; she has no other escape. Otherwise, she will die and with her will perish all her dreams and unfaded hopes. She weeps. "I don't want to die, there's still so much to do. I haven't done anything wrong. I haven't killed anyone. I haven't made a mistake. Why should I pay for other people's failings? Why does everyone end up taking advantage of me? Why is this happening to me and not to other women? Is that question so difficult that no one can answer it? I don't want to die. I don't want to die just for being a woman. Only God decides when we die. I don't want to die. My only mistake was to have been honest, to have trusted. I was just too naïve. I don't want to die. It's not fair. I have a right to be happy. I don't want to die, I don't want to, I don't want to..."

Yet however much she cries, however unfair it all seems, her family or husband's family will carry on searching. And if they find her, she will fall victim to the gunshot wounds of custom, tradition, and sexism. There will be no escape.

Zelal recovers her composure. She has aged beyond her thirty-two years, her face withered by distress and sadness. Yet surprisingly, her eyes still sparkle like freshly polished gems. It must be from so many tears.

"I'll survive, like I've always done. I'm not afraid. I'll fly to Germany and there I'll find my way. They'll give me a visa and I'll go to university; after that I'll work. I'll be independent; I'll never need any dammed men. I'll do it. I'm convinced. I'll make it. I believe in myself." The inner strength of this woman, who has been raped, beaten, and abused, emerges now like that of a wounded lion that refuses to be hunted. Then she shatters into a thousand pieces, a mirror never again to be put right. Once more, the terrified young woman reappears. Doubts suddenly take shape; her destiny, plagued by ill fate, overwhelms her. She breaks down. "If I don't get the visa, I'll have to confront them, go back to my town. Face up and tell them to kill me because I can't stand it any more. I'm sick of running. I'm tired of feeling scared to death every time I hear footsteps behind me. I don't want to dodge them between the stalls or suffer more panic attacks. I can't cope with more lies, with this weight bearing down on me. That's my final decision. It doesn't make sense to carry on living like this. It's not worth it. At least I'll die with my family."

"I don't want this life!" she shouts, as if those words of child-like rage could pave the way for a world of colour. Yet she does not belong there. Hers is a world painted black-and-white, where greys or different shades find no refuge.

As if by magic, the thousand shards of glass once again form a mirror and the other woman now appears. The woman who is aware of her rights and the opportunities the world has to offer. She speaks with confidence, assurance, and hatred, and she issues a threat.

"They used me, now I'll use them. I'm going to take advantage, I'll take his money, I'll get out of here and then I'll be free once and for all. I'll have to be strong, but afterwards I'll feel proud of my self. I know I will. I'll live."

Two minutes later she falls to pieces once again.

"Too many people are after me: my ex-husband, my family, Emin. I have no chance unless I get away from this country, this city that I hate. I'll die."

What angers her the most is to imagine leaving this world without having loved. All she knows of love is contained in the lyrics of the songs she hums constantly. She has never loved and this grieves her terribly. "Perhaps I'll fall in love with the ground that covers me when I'm dead," she says, taking a cruel delight in her own unhappiness.

Worse still, she cannot recall a single moment in her life when she felt happy. Every minute of her thirty-two years has been marked with pain; even the birth of her children was stripped of joy by the beatings.

She is no longer safe. For a year and a half she was, but it is over. She was brought up never to look behind her, not as an attitude to the past, but because men could take it as an invitation. Recently, however, she has been constantly turning around to see if anyone is there; if her moment has come, if the agony is over.

Zelal, it turns out, really has done something wrong. Something so vile as to merit this death sentence, this punishment that will serve as an example to others. What was this terrible offence? Well, she dared to get a divorce. The woman, who today deserves to die, filed for—and even worse, achieved—a legal separation from her husband.

And in many parts of southeastern Turkey, this is paid for with one's life. Because there, something exists that is above all else, most of all above women, who are worthless. Something more valuable than the land no longer theirs, than the possessions they no longer own, than the money long since vanished. That something determines life, regulates social relationships, and keeps women in line. That something is called HONOUR, and people kill for it.

2

Killed by a Phone Call, Rape, and Gossip...

Staining the honour of one's family or husband—to lay waste their good name, to trample it with cheerful disregard—is the worst thing a woman can do in southeastern Turkey, a region whose inhabitants, beset by poverty, unemployment, and war, are left with only one thing: their dignity. Discrediting the clan brings terrible consequences because respect from one's neighbours is fundamental in traditional Anatolia, where the population remains firmly rooted to their customs, their traditions, and their *Töre* (the age-old laws governing social relationships).

So, those who dare to contravene these rules will die. These are the so-called honour crimes (*Namus Cinayetleri*), which occur all too frequently in twenty-first century Turkey and are usually perpetrated by the family of the victim herself. Honour (*namus*) is intimately linked with women's sexuality,[1] with chastity. In fact, this virtue is interpreted so broadly that even the most insignificant thing can be cause for murder: showing one's legs, neck, or hands, or simply the style of dress. Even a voice is enough to destroy a family's reputation. Such was the case of a young woman killed at the hands of her brothers: a man used to phone her constantly, which had given rise to local gossip.[2] The girl was guilty of nothing but picking up the handset.

Rumours among female neighbours, who spread insults and kill time with tittle-tattle, are all that is required to drag a family's good name through the mud. It is enough to call a radio station and request a love song. In Turkey, this has already been cause for murder. A teenager from Urfa, who just wanted to listen to some romantic lyrics, ended up being killed when this sentimental desire was linked to the notion that she may have a lover.

Everything has the potential to result in an honour crime, although the leading cause is disobeying family orders, be that refusing to marry someone, complaining about one's husband, or even—incredibly—not wanting to have sex with one's father or brother-in-law. A young woman will also pay with her life if she is raped or abused.[3] More often than one would expect, stories emerge of rape committed by family members against girls just fourteen years old, later killed by their own fathers to recover the family's honour. Even worse, if in addition to "letting herself be raped" the victim becomes pregnant, then there really is no escape. The remarkable drama of poor Güldünya, who became pregnant after being sexually assaulted by a distant relative, serves to prove this point. Her brothers followed her to Istanbul, where the twenty-two-year-old had taken refuge from the forked tongues of her village and given birth to her baby. In the streets of ancient Byzantium, the two young men, only twenty and twenty-four years old, attempted to put an end to their sister's life. Their bullets, however, ended up in her leg. It was later in the hospital where she was convalescing, recovering from her wounds when they finished off the job. Two gunshots in the head would be the tragic climax of Güldünya's escape and of negligence by a police force already alerted to the family's intentions.

Even simple visual contact with a man or fleeing home to avoid one's fate is paid for with a torment befitting the most harrowing dramas. Without any shadow of a doubt, having sexual relations before marriage, being unfaithful to one's husband, or eloping with a lover are all considered by this society as just cause to commit murder.

How do women know what could lead them to an early grave? The fine line separating what is honourable from that which can shroud a family in shame is only visible to those who have grown up within the household. Even then, family members themselves can sometimes be taken by surprise. Women must sound out their parents to discover what they can and cannot do, though in many cases this is insufficient, as the family's social environment also has a part to play.[4]

It is estimated that 231 honour crimes were committed in Turkey in 2007, although this data is unreliable and the real figure may be much higher.[1] Between 2003 and 2007 the number of murders committed under the banner of "respectability" reached over 1,100.[5]

The large cities, focus points for immigrants from the southeast, today provide the backdrop for the most callous and lethal stories. In fact, crimes committed in the name of honour have doubled in Istanbul: in 2007 one person per week died a victim of score settling to re-establish the dignity of a humiliated family.[2] These crimes are also typical of the least-developed areas of rural Turkey, the region bordering Syria, Iran, and Iraq; a society characterised by its patriarchal and sexist nature.

There, honour is everything. A kind of everything that is cleansed much quicker than it is sullied. Before the victim's blood has dried, the family is free of all stain. Yesterday, no one greeted them, they were scorned; today, after murdering their daughter, they are once again respectable members of society. Honour is recovered with the same swiftness as bullets issued from a shotgun. Honour is everything.

---

1 The frequency with which honour crimes occur is difficult to determine, most of all if one takes into account that some crimes are disguised as suicides and other murders are not even reported as the victim was not registered at birth.

2 Over the past five years, there have been 167 crimes in Istanbul (15%), 144 in Ankara (13%), in Izmir 121 (11%) and 69 in Diyarbakir. Killings in the name of honour doubled in Istanbul from 2006 to 2007: in 2006 there were 26 and in 2007, 53.

3

The Most Dissuasive Measure: the Shotgun

Zelal perfectly recalls the first time they tried to kill her. It was almost two years ago, yet the faces of her brothers-in-law, prepared to mete out punishment, remain all too fresh in her memory. She had served them food every day for over four years, though her efforts had not once been met with thanks. Now, those same young men, who had never uttered a positive word about a single dish, would become her executioners.

Loitering in that square, like hunters lying in wait, their intentions were perfectly clear; they were two men willing to do whatever was necessary. When she saw them, Zelal froze to her very soul. She was expecting them, but not so soon. Only a week had passed since receiving the divorce decree, only seven days of freedom. But liberty came at a price. Zelal was aware of that, and her brothers-in-law were here as a reminder. Perhaps they never wished it to reach this point. Who knows? What is clear is that they had tried to put her off from the start. Now, however, there was no alternative left but to punish the stubbornness of that "stupid" woman who had opted for divorce, risking and casting doubt on the family's good name.

First, it was her husband who had tried to dissuade her with suicide threats, appealing to the blighted conscience of his wife who, in his own peculiar, sadistic, and indifferent way, he had always adored. From prison, he threw into confusion the two different women who still inhabited Zelal's body, making them fight it out, battle between themselves once more. Zelal felt sorry for him but had discovered that violence was a vicious circle, endlessly repeating itself, and that its perpetrators suffered a weakness as incurable as it was destructive.

Then came the threats and intimidation against the lawyers working on the case; defiant words charged with real danger. The family even sent two thugs to ensure that these warnings got results. Effective they were, and on two occasions the legal team threw in their robes, taking refuge in less risky cases. None of them was willing to sport with death; they were in southeastern Anatolia, and nobody there doubts an ultimatum of this calibre.

Finally, a lawyer appeared who would not succumb to the pressure, along with a judge who took pity on the young woman. It was not so difficult, given that four members of her husband's family, including himself, were in prison. The judge would always be left with a doubt whether, in signing that divorce, he was at the same time sentencing the young woman to death.

Now there remained the most dissuasive measure of all: the shotgun. Her husband's brothers were waiting for her in that square armed with the weapon of custom, of tradition, of honour. They shouted her name, which resounded inside her troubled mind, setting off alarm signals within milliseconds. She saw them coming but hijacked by fear, her short, stocky frame remained riveted to the spot. Etched in her memory are the faces of those who had never been pleasant but were certainly familiar, recognisable. Her mind was bombarded by images in fast motion, snapshots of them in different situations. Four years living in the same household linked her to those men. Terror then regained its place in the young woman's mind, dragging her back to the crowded square. Gasping for breath, her hands trembling, Zelal was completely unable to move. She had got off the bus, just taken the stop in the city centre, walked only a few steps and now...those men. She did not know what to do.

"They can't kill me here in front of everyone." This thought comforted her for a second but doubts immediately rushed in. "Or can they?"

As the silhouettes became more visible, more clearly defined, so too did the bulges in the sides of their jackets. Little imagination was required to perceive the outline of a weapon. Zelal could make out the butts of the pistols stuffed into her relative's trousers and this finally shook her into action, suddenly bringing home the vital need to get away as quickly as possible.

Movement returned to her limbs, which now became agile. She ran, chased by the two men who had abandoned their slow but sure pace. The labyrinth of shops, stalls, and crisscrossing alleyways was perfectly familiar, providing hundreds of potential hiding places. She did not stop. Her mind was blank, she could sense nothing but the agitated breathing from her own exhausted body. The headscarf perhaps made her easier to spot among the crowd, but it is impossible to recall.

Zelal carried on running, slipping down winding backstreets, leaving the crowd behind, not knowing whether she had managed to shake off her pursuers, not once looking back to check. If they were going to kill her, she preferred not to see it. She would turn her back to them, as girls were brought up to do.

Unconsciously, she headed towards the only safe refuge in the midst of those alleyways: the offices of a women's organisation where she helped out. Along the way, Zelal must have thrown off the two men because when she finally made it, crossed into the doorway, called the lift, and stopped, struggling for breath, no one pounced.

Suddenly, a couple of voices set her on alert once again. Struggling to listen, she discovered that the sound coming from the stairway was that of women chatting. More precisely, two different tones of voice, both familiar to her: two colleagues she had been working with over the past five months. They were fully aware of the situation. In fact, they had encouraged Zelal to file for divorce and provided psychological support. They were also her friends; right now, the only people she could trust. No explanation was needed; her expression alone revealed the gravity of the situation.

"They're here," was the only thing she managed to say.

They climbed the narrow staircase and arrived at the office, where tending to women in trouble was nothing out of the ordinary.

The escape plan had been designed some time ago, as no one had any doubt that, at some point, this day would come. To think otherwise would have been reckless, if not stupid. The only thing they needed to do now was bring that plan forward.

First, Zelal must leave the city as soon as possible. They connected to the Internet and started the online search for her ticket to salvation. She would fly to Ankara, the first stop on a journey back to square one. With the ticket in her hand, she called her supposed benefactor—the same man who would later exploit her—to bring him up to date on the new situation. They agreed that a widower's family would pick up Zelal in the Turkish capital, take her to a town close to Istanbul, and look after her until the man of the house arrived. She only had to collect her belongings.

Meanwhile, her brothers-in-law continued searching for her all over town, guns at the ready. They had approval from the family and, most of all, from Zelal's husband, who was still in prison.

Shielding herself from fear with the help of a couple of friends, Zelal reached the police station. There, in line with the plan rushed forward by the premature unfolding of events, she had already applied for the passport, which would temporarily free her from those who were on her trail.

It was nighttime when she reached her parents' home. Within five minutes her few belongings were packed, thrown into cases with the haste and carelessness of one who does not have a second to lose. Once again, she left her former home; in the end, the only place where, despite being treated with contempt, she had never fallen victim to men's brute force. A female friend would provide her next refuge.

Nervousness, dread, and distrust all slept with Zelal that night, the last she would spend in her home city. Enveloped in doubt, menaced by the nightmare ahead, anguished by the lie that her life would become.

The half-light of a different house, that of her friend, became the canvass upon which a picture of her life took shape; an ill-formed sketch, a collection of stains. She was tormented by the same question: why? Why me? There were enough hours that night for this question to repeat itself in her mind all too many times without finding a single convincing answer, or one that could help her to accept her role as prey, about to be devoured by the wolves of tradition.

Morning brought back her real and palpable nightmare. Her brothers-in-law had gone to the women's organisation offices, asking for her and making threats. There was no doubt: she had to leave.

4

Three Suicide Attempts

As with Zelal's story, in most honour killings the decision to murder a woman is taken by none other than the family council.[1] Only men play a part in this lethal assembly: father, brothers, uncles, cousins, even the victim's sons. Women, as usual, are kept out, unless they are going through menopause. In this case, they are considered to have a more masculine attitude and are given the right to vote. Although they suffer and on occasion have attempted to intercede for their children, even alerting their daughters to aid escape, mothers are obliged to obey. The majority support the decisions taken by the men as their reputation as a member of the household is also at risk.[2]

Father and relatives do not only sentence "the erring girl" to death, but also plot how to get rid of her and choose who will be the one to carry out punishment. In some cases, it is the head of the family; otherwise, the woman's brothers or, if they dare not, then cousins or uncles. Women die, then, at the hands of their own families.

---

1 The sentence is issued by the woman's family in 35% of cases and in 34.8%, by the man's family.

2 Women are not supported by their families in 76% of cases.

To make matters worse, they are victims of their youngest relatives—sometimes less than fourteen years old—who, until the new Turkish penal code came into force in 2005, benefitted from greatly reduced sentences because of their age. These adolescents do not hesitate to carry out their task; they will spend only a few years behind bars—two or three, at most—and, more importantly, win the family's admiration and respect. Not to do it would be to ostracise themselves completely. Some openly confess in court that they have cleansed their honour; in return, they will obtain much-desired social prestige, which outweighs the pain of losing a mother, sister, or cousin. While these young men bathe in glory, their victims lie in their tombs, unavenged in the face of such dire injustice.

However, the children forced to commit these crimes are themselves victims; victims of their own families, society, traditions, and upbringing. Much as it may grieve them, they endure this task with the same stoicism as women affront the housework and the beatings. It is their duty to cleanse the family's honour, as it is the women's duty to polish the doorframe.

Women are shot, have their throats cut, are poisoned, stoned, or pushed down wells. In one case, a girl was even crushed to death under a tractor, only for her killer to later claim in court that it had been an accident. She had returned home after running away with a man her family had promised to let her marry. They forced the young woman onto the truck without wasting a second. When she realised what they were planning, she tried to escape but fortune was not on her side. The eldest of her brothers ran straight over her, crushing every bone in her body under the tractor's enormous wheels. It's not exactly the lightest of vehicles.

Another very common method is to tie a woman's hands and feet, then throw her into a river. Tradition dictates that if the victim is able to untie herself and escape, then she is clean. Otherwise, the family is shown to be completely justified in executing her. As one might imagine, in 100 percent of these cases the fatal outcome vindicates the family's decision.[6]

Turkish laws were tightened in 2005, with family members being charged if they obliged children to murder. As a result, the clans have opted to pressure young women themselves, forcing them to take their own lives.[1] This devious approach means that no one goes to jail yet sets right the affront to a family's dignity. In this way, honour killings are disguised as common suicides.

"You have brought shame on this family. Kill yourself and cleanse our honour. Otherwise, we will do it." This was the text message that seventeen-year-old Deyra received on her mobile. Her sin? To have fallen for a guy that she chatted to regularly by phone.

Fear and a feeling of guilt led the teenager to follow her family's instructions without hesitation. She tried to kill herself three times, though it seems that she was destined to live. The first time, she threw herself into the biblical Tigris River. On that day, good fortune came in the shape of a policeman who rescued her from the icy waters. In a second attempt, she made a noose, tied it to the living room ceiling, and let herself fall from the sofa. Her uncle took pity on the motionless body suspended in the air and rushed his niece to hospital. Deyra believed herself to be such a sinner, so worthy of her fate, that she devised a third plan to end her life. This time she cut her wrists with a kitchen knife. Yet fate was still on Deyra's side. In the end, she turned to a women's organisation in Batman (southeastern Turkey)[7] for protection and now lives in hiding.

Those who manage to carry out their parents' orders not only die but also cover up for the real killers before the law. Unless the case falls into the hands of a public prosecutor keen to investigate, the crime will go unpunished. Once again, the murders get away with it and the women are left to weep, suffer, and perish, convinced that they are to blame.

A young woman is given a rope, taken to a barn, and forced to end her own life while the family waits outside. In one such case, a broken chair leg prevented the "undesirable" from hanging herself, and the girl—who, like many in these cases, considered herself guilty and deserving of punishment—ran out to her family in tears, convinced that she was an even greater sinner for being unable to carry out her own sentence.[8] If it were not enough to be raped, abused, or forced to die, women are psychologically destroyed, torn to shreds, and made to kill themselves.

---

1 14.6% of women are forced to commit suicide.

Sometimes, though rarely, macabre agreements can save lives. For example, if a woman is raped and so no longer a virgin, the solution is to marry her to the rapist. In this way, the damaged goods are off loaded. If she is already married, then in order to restore her husband's honour he may be offered one of the rapist's daughters in matrimony. The rape victim is left alone, at the mercy of her own family, who may then decide to kill her.

If a girl has had sexual relations before marriage then it may be decided that she wed a member of the family. Alternatively, she may be offered to an older man as a second wife, so covering up the stain on the family's good name.

It is extremely difficult, however, to find a negotiated solution that does not require blood to be spilt if a woman's only crime is to have shown her hair or been the object of completely unfounded gossip among neighbours.

5

The Washing Machine and the Blood

She was named Zelal, though had it been for her father she wouldn't even have been given a name; they would simply have referred to her by her gender, because, unfortunately, she was born a woman or, to be more exact, she was born a female where she shouldn't have been. In a province of southeastern Turkey like any other, in a neighbourhood like any other, in a Kurdish family like any other, where women's value is still determined by the price paid for them when given in marriage. Before and after that day they are worthless.[1] They are

[1] A man pays for the woman he marries an amount known as the "bride-price" compensation to the woman's family for the cost of raising her and the loss of valuable services she provided within the household. Of course, this money is paid for a chaste woman, a virgin. If a family wishes to keep the value of their goods intact, they should make every effort to keep her pure. Damaged goods can be returned, killed, abandoned or repudiated. It is not only sexual relations before marriage that can ruin a woman's life forever, but also being unable to bear children. In this case, the husband may even acquire another wife, which the first is forced to live with. Although polygamy has been banned in Turkey since 1926, it still persists in regions where traditions are maintained. Moreover, taking into account that according to the Qur'an – as it is interpreted in these areas – more than one wife is allowed as long as the husband is able to maintain them.

spirits that drift through life serving meals and producing children. And woe betide those who make themselves noticed!

Zelal was completely disregarded, to such an extent that it was not until her fifth birthday that she discovered who was really her father. She had never called him "Dad," and he had always ignored her, an invisible spectre wandering around the house. Only at this point did her make-believe father recover his true role as older brother.

From that day onward, Zelal would hide away and watch her male relatives enjoying games with her recently discovered father, adding even more pain to the suffering of this young woman, orphaned in spirit. Her mother had been unable to endure the beatings from the man who supposedly loved her; the physical abuse that comes with being a woman in a land governed by the laws of men. One day, before her daughter had even reached two months of age, she took her own life. This is nothing out of the ordinary in these parts.

Zelal was lucky enough to attend school in a region where women are often denied the right to education.[1] However, her gaze always had to be focussed on the ground. Even before she could speak, Zelal already knew that she was not allowed to look at men and that her attitude should be demure, to say the very least. "Don't speak, don't dishonour us, you're a girl," were the words echoed in her mind as if it were an empty vault. And now she really does believe that her mind was indeed vacant, that despite all the classes attended over the years, she was no more than an educated fool. She adopted the mental echoes of her family's ideas as her very own, without realising that their only objective was to serve as a straightjacket, to keep the outside world from her, to keep the unruly horse contained. She knew nothing of her rights as a woman; that women could legitimately make decisions, travel, communicate, or establish relationships like

[1] Despite huge efforts on the part of the government and media, there are still women who do not access education in these rural areas. Some are unable to write, let alone use the Internet. What is more, some 19% of women in these parts cannot speak Turkish, the country's official language. They only speak Kurdish, a banned language in which it is impossible to carry out any type of dealing beyond their social environment, even less report to the authorities any violation of their most basic rights.

any other human being. And she knew even less about anything related to sex, let alone contraceptive methods.

You can't speak, you can't laugh, you can't express your feelings, you can't leave the house; a long list of prohibitions which, at that time, seem logical. After all, weren't they just the same for all the women she knew?

For Zelal, there would be no teenage love affairs, stolen glances, or heart-to-hearts with the girls. She knew that a simple look could bring about a tragedy. The family rules were very clear and death would be the certain punishment for anyone who dared to disobey. Not once did Zelal glance upward, fearful of a future that would turn out to be even crueller than she had imagined.

She never heard her friends talk about their boyfriends, nor did she see lovers kissing on TV, as the girls would be ordered to get up from the sofa and leave the room first. However, her snub nose, lively brown eyes, and rounded figure—a petite frame vying with the fullness of her thighs—did not escape Mehmet's attention, the man who had no hesitation in threatening to burn down Zelal's home and kill her family if she did not accept him in marriage. And they call that love! Tribes such as those of her fiery admirer were dangerous, Zelal knew that much. These were not empty threats launched into the wind.

The household just across the street served as an example. Zelal's neighbour had rejected one of Mehmet's cousins, who was intent on marrying her, and this refusal was met with gunshots. Resistance was futile. She was not fatally wounded, and after an operation and a long period of recovery, finally resigned herself to her fate.

"You'll be mine or you'll die," was the declaration of love from the man who would, in the end, become Zelal's husband and take her to a life of beatings and abuse in Istanbul.

She was twenty-three when she left home, wearing her wedding dress. She now wonders if ever she manages to return, whether it will be in white once again, wrapped in a wretched Muslim funeral shroud, the *kefen*.

Her husband's love took the shape of lashings with a belt, the occasional caress, and sexual abuse, all encouraged by a mother-in-law who was of the old-school opinion that "women are for beating and making children." The bruises and battery were accompanied by ill treatment and humiliation suffered at the hands of her husband's family. Zelal became the family's girl—the *gelin*—who, more than daughter-in-law or sister-in-law, was the clan's slave. She would do the cooking and then wait until everyone had finished—she wasn't allowed to sit at the table—to eat the leftovers from their plates. They never let her sit on the sofa to watch TV; she was only permitted to sit on a chair or on the floor by the door in case anyone wanted anything.

On the European side of Istanbul, Zelal lived in an apartment along with the fifteen people who made up the family nucleus. By the time it was her turn to take a shower, there was no warm water left, even in the freezing cold winter mornings when the pungent scent of humanity often pervades the city's streets. The whole family took decisions on Zelal's future, even gave their opinion on how many times her husband should have sex with her or how she should dress: wide, ankle-length skirts were her uniform because only "whores" wear trousers. Of course, her shoulder-length auburn hair covered with an Islamic headscarf. Her voice counted for nothing; it was nonexistent, devoid of all sound. She was not a person but a slave, a skivvy who did not deserve to have a single lira in her pocket. When she gave birth to her two children, she was suffering from hunger. Later, she would feed them water and sugar to stave off the malnutrition that comes with poverty.

Faced with his own inability to find work, her husband's method of letting off steam was to beat his wife then ask his brother-in-law for money to keep her. Though she knew nothing of these payments, she was painfully aware of the abuse. He would hit her violently and she would keep quiet, like the good Kurdish woman she was. Resisting or even calling the police would have only made her feel worse; involving the authorities is not honourable and would have brought nothing but further humiliation.

Zelal endured four years of abuse until the very author of this violence finally took pity on her, faced with the image of her body stretched out on the floor in a pool of blood. He had hit her so hard that she was completely unable to move. Tormented with guilt, he took her back, temporarily, to the home of some relatives in Istanbul so that they could look after her.

Zelal watched the washing machine incessantly spinning, her clothes inside drenched in blood, her feelings in turmoil. She searched deep within herself, beyond what she had learned, to conclude that this situation was intolerable. No longer would she endure the searing pain of his belt, the punches, the abuse. The old Zelal died that day and remained in limbo for two years before returning, reincarnated in a new woman, a Zelal who was aware of her rights.

She returned to her roots, to her hometown. Her father had died and her stepmother, far from the fairy-tale villain, was a docile woman who would nurse her through her recovery. Leaving Istanbul with her step-brothers, Zelal's thoughts turned to her children. She would never see them again.

6

The Martyrs

However you look at it, women are the martyrs of the Turkish society in which Zelal was raised. They are the victims of beatings and stabbings but also of a mind-set educated in honour that makes them feel guilty for their behaviour and deserving of punishment; this forces them to support the murder of their daughters, to consent when their sisters are killed, and to accept in silence when they lose their mothers. They are even made to become their own executioners, tying the noose to hang themselves or initiating the lethal gossip that will be their neighbours' downfall.

Martyrs persecuted in the name of honour have a similar profile: women who have no education, who have children, who do not work outside the home, and who hail from backgrounds where one of their female relatives has been killed or forced to commit suicide over issues related to the family's dignity.[1] They are usually Kurds and feel the need to be protected by men, who they are duty bound to listen to and obey. If that were not enough, they consider it acceptable for

[1] 79% of women in these circumstances have children, 91% do not work and 55% have no education, according to a study carried out by the Kamer Association among women who applied to them for help. *Who's to blame? 2005*. Kamer Report.

men to beat them. This is the upbringing they have received, what they have witnessed in their homes since childhood, and is so normal in their eyes that it seems both fair and proper.[9]

Girls who become women far too soon, in a society afflicted by poverty, war, and feudalism. Most are forced to marry young. Some are wed at the tender age of just thirteen or fourteen, though this is forbidden under Turkish law.[1] Religious ceremonies are held, which are not officially legal without the civil union, and before the girl has given up playing with her dolls she will already have a husband on her arm and a real baby to keep her entertained.

Here, as in every aspect of their lives, women have absolutely no say. Although they are sometimes listened to, the decisions taken by their elders are irreversible. To make matters worse, they inhabit an area in constant upheaval because of the armed conflict with the Kurdistan Workers' Party (PKK), the Kurdish rebels fighting against the Turkish authorities for an independent state.

Along with rape, beatings, harassment, and forced marriage, women suffer the deaths of their sons and brothers at the hands of the Turkish army or Kurdish insurgents. Interestingly, some women decide to take to the mountains and become guerrilla fighters and it is there, not in their homes, where they find freedom. In the mountains—thanks to the influence of the Marxist ideas underpinning this group, led by Abdullah Öcalan—women can enjoy the very same status as men.

---

[1] Under the new Civil Code, the legal age for marriage is 18. Prior to 2001 it was 15.

7

The New Zelal

She lived in limbo. For over two years she remained in a catatonic state, a puppet without a will of her own, at life's mercy. What she most cherished had been left behind in Istanbul, the city she now loathed. All her past life had died there.

She wiled away the hours at her home, in a village of southeastern Turkey, reliving each of the four years spent in the big city and, most of all, remembering the children she had lost. Her mother-in-law had taken charge and she would never see them again. "What will they have told my little ones?" she wondered. "Will they say that I abandoned them? For sure, they won't explain my reasons," she answered herself.

Obsessively, hopelessly, Zelal brooded on her two young boys, miserable at having left them. She had managed to retrieve one of her younger son's socks, which she now clutched to her chest; it had become her comforter, without which she was unable to sleep. It was impossible for her to see TV cartoons or anything related to children. She could not bear to go into shops that sold children's clothes, and every time she saw a mother hand-in-hand with her child, she turned her head away for fear of entering a state of shock.

She felt miserable. And she was miserable, though for the first time in many years her body was not covered in bruises, unsightly marks blemishing her pale skin. Zelal was still unable to understand what she had done to deserve so many beatings. Now, alone, she regretted having endured this abuse for such a long time. Her only mistake had been to remain silent for too long, not saying a word, submissively taking each blow with the feeling that she was at fault, surrendering to a destiny that showed her no mercy.

Having locked herself into a micro-universe limited by the walls of her stepmother's home, Zelal retreated within herself, constantly turning things over in her mind. Not for a single second did she cast her gaze outwards. The outside world was an even harsher reminder of the children she had borne and this caused her more pain than the darkness deep inside.

As far as her local community was concerned, Zelal's escape from her marital home was completely masked by the events that unfolded after she left. Even the least significant of her neighbours knew that her husband had been sent to prison and would spend the next four years behind bars for murdering his father. The man had been condemned to death by a family council for having forced his wife into prostitution. What people did not know was that Mehmet killed his father four months after Zelal had managed to escape. If she had still been with her husband, she would never have let him become the executing arm of this ruthless family, which did not hesitate to solve all its problems with a shotgun.

It would not have been difficult to justify the absence of Zelal's children either, given her precarious financial situation and the possibility that they could remain with her mother-in-law. So, in the interests of her own safety, no one in the village was made aware of Zelal's real situation.

At some point during that period of lethargy, somewhere inside her deepest fears, loneliness, incomprehension, pain, longing, fear, paralysis, monotony, and rejection, she decided—or was convinced—to try out a new route. Armed with courage, she turned to other women for help, to one organisation in particular. They could, perhaps, put back together the shattered Zelal, rebuild her broken psyche, create a new person from the ashes of the woman who had watched transfixed as a washing machine had spun with her own blood.

"A Kurdish woman should never turn to those groups, just like they should never go to the police. It's not well seen by society but I did it," she recalls. "I did it because it was the only thing I could do if I didn't want to die inside."

She was placed in the care of the centre's psychologist, who prepared the ground upon which to construct the new Zelal. They started with the most basic foundation—her sense of self-worth—and demolished the preconceptions and limitations that her own mind, educated in gender inequality, had built up through force of habit. One day she learnt that women had rights and that these were not something abstract but were written down in a document called the Constitution. On another occasion they explained that women are of equal value as men and that the two worlds she had created in her mind—a superior space, inhabited by men and another, inferior, where women scratched out an existence—were nothing more than a product of a society. Of her society, but not the only reality in the world. She could not believe her ears when she was told that women also have a say when it comes to sex.

Zelal realised then that she had been a prisoner; from now on, she would no longer be forced to endure such a life. Courage blossomed within her and she learnt not to cry because crying would achieve nothing. Working and gaining economic independence, that was the secret to female happiness.

Nine months of psychological support and fast-track courses in human rights finally brought a new Zelal into the world. Yet inside her, fragments of the other woman remained like splinters piercing deep within her body, impossible to remove.

Like everything in Zelal's life, it happened with an air of tragicomedy, the next instalment in a series of Hollywood blockbusters. A new character appeared on the scene who was to bring more tension and further instability. He would take advantage of the weaknesses that a therapy of just nine months had not been able to overcome. Emine was the name of the man who fashioned himself as Zelal's saviour. And although the psychological treatment had convinced her that the opposite sex was of no use and that it was preferable to deal with things for herself, the other Zelal ended up allowing herself to fall into the protective arms of this much older man, who was almost sixty.

The strangest thing, however, was the way they met. One day, Zelal dialled a wrong number in Germany. She wanted to speak to her brother, who had been living there for some time, but it was a Turkish widower who picked up the phone. Emine, a man who, in his solitude, listened to that woman's words, her story, her explanations, and declared himself her benefactor. One phone call led to another. In the era of new communications technology, Turkish people too fall in love in cyberspace. Not in Zelal's village though.

Emine went to visit and promised to get her out of there, to free her from the precarious situation in which she found herself. What Zelal did not know was that she would pass from being the possession of one man to become the property of another, nothing more. Naivety and the only chance of a way out prevailed over prudence and independence.

It was then, against a constant ebb and flow of doubt, that the decision she used to make only to change it a few seconds later, finally became firm. She had discussed it with her new friends from the association and now that prohibited, unthinkable idea was gaining strength in her mind. She was well aware of the possible consequences but with the help of those women, together with the man who promised to support her, she would evade the family council's verdict. The time had come to take control of her life and put into practice those rights that she had heard so much about: she would get a divorce, conscious it could cost her life.

With the decree absolute in her hand, on Valentine's Day, 2006, it really registered that her rights had triumphed in a society where this never seemed to occur. Although practically no one knew—it could lead to a battle between the clans of each family—that deep-down feeling of having achieved the first victory in her life was enough. She felt proud of herself, strong, invincible, and able to face anything. She would no longer be the family's slave but, as a counterweight, would spend the rest of her life watching her back. More than once, she would be forced to flee, armed men chasing after her. There was no doubt in her mind; it was worth it and she would fight them. This was her triumph, achieved almost single-handed. It is true that her family had supported her. But they would never have done so had they known of the plan she contrived to escape those who were to pursue her from that day forth.

All of these projects were cut short, however, when her brothers-in-law turned up much sooner than she had imagined, ready to put an end to her life. They did not give her time to put the finishing touches to a plan that was to free her from one lion's cage only to imprison her in another. Newer, shinier, but at the end of the day still a cage.

While she ran, while she fled, attempting to camouflage herself among the crowd, to disappear down alleyways, she came to the realisation that, even so, this was better than eating other people's leftovers, washing their clothes, and enduring physical abuse, and more revealing still, that this was not her day to die. For once, the expert in reading coffee grounds—accurately unravelling life's mysteries for others but never for herself—had a flash of intuition about her own fate that was absolutely right.

She managed to slip away on that occasion but the time had come to escape forever. The agreement was as follows: the director of the women's organisation, with whom she had worked side by side over the last five months, would make it known that Zelal had been appointed to run a project working with European institutions, based in France. From now on, she would reside there and only occasionally return to Turkey to attend conferences.

The real plan, however, was much less sophisticated and more characteristic of a Kurdish woman like Zelal than this idealised scheme, fruit of an imagination completely out of synch with her reality. Emine, the man she had only just met, would accept responsibility for her. He would take her to a village thousands of kilometres from her home, where she would be difficult to find, with a promise that, at some point in the future, he would find a way to get her out of the country.

That day, saying good-bye to her family at the airport, Zelal did not know what the next few years would bring. She was conscious, however, that these kisses could be the last they would exchange and that the same people who were now embracing her could become her murderers. It was the first time that she had lied to them and from that day onward she would do so continuously, with fake phone calls from the home of this man who was to become her lover. No family in southeastern Turkey would allow such deception to go unpunished. As she boarded the plane, Zelal notched up one more on the list of justifications for her own murder.

8

Cleanse Your Honour, Then You Can Talk

Society in southeastern Turkey can itself be responsible for murder: it does not bear the weapon but it points to the victim. It condemns young women to death without the least consideration. Devoid of sentimentality, society pressures families to take desperate measures in order to recover the dignity they have supposedly lost. It is considered to be ultimately responsible for these women and, as such, issues its sentence.[1]

If the family does not comply, its members will be condemned to the cruellest ostracism in a population where community and social relations are everything. The baker will refuse to sell them the indispensable Turkish bread because their daughter has run away with a lad from the village; the grocer will not let a family marked by such lack of decorum buy his vegetables. Neighbours will no longer greet them, people will spit on them, they will be bombarded with phrases

---

1 In a survey carried out in south-eastern Turkey, respondents considered it society's duty to not look the other way (18.4%), keep an eye on women who live in their street or neighbourhood (12.3%), protect the *töre* (12.5) or did not consider that they had any duty (12.3%). *Who's to blame?* Kamer Report 2005.

such as "Go and cleanse you honour first," "Haven't you finished off your whore yet?" and, "First, recover your honour, then you can talk."[10]

The family will be the target of mockery within the community, the object of rumour and gossip whenever they pass by. At school, the household's youngest members will be exposed to the ever-innocent comments from other children about the sister who has robbed them of their dignity. Meanwhile, other relatives will be unable to find work, always for the same reason. Although they may not wish to kill, although families allow themselves to be swayed by emotional and blood ties, in the end it is less painful to rid themselves of that member who dishonours them all.

Despite this, there are families that do not give in, who will not agree to murder their daughters. The only option then is to abandon their home and move to another province, leaving behind their roots, land, and the friends who now turn their backs on them. And herein lies another tragedy, given that in this society a person has no worth as an individual, only as part of the group to which they belong. In southeastern Turkey, the bonds between members of a clan or tribe are so tight, so essential for the individual's existence that to find oneself outside these groups is practically to die. Society, then, forces families to balance the love for their children against their dignity.

The community is so powerful that, by spreading rumours, it can also create motives for murder; it even acts as an accomplice. Local society closes its eyes or looks the other way when crimes are committed right under people's noses. In village streets or town squares, women have had their throats cut in full view of the grocer, the water seller, the fruit vendor, and the butcher, and all claim not to have seen anything. Each of them was busy doing their own thing while a girl was ruthlessly executed before their very eyes. That is what happened to Sevda, a young woman murdered by her fourteen-year-old cousin because she enjoyed going out for walks and no one wanted to marry her. The teenager slit her throat in front of everyone, yet no one testified against him in court. In the end, he spent less than three years in prison.

A lack of education, religious ignorance, isolation, and war shape the character of these communities in southeastern Turkey. If one adds the dearth in basic economic resources, which prevents them from reaching a more open culture or overcoming the patriarchal system and clan organisation, the Molotov cocktail is served. Marginalised and far removed from state support, they believe that the only thing which can help them survive is to continue as always, with these rules governing relationships between extended families, united by blood ties and sentimental bonds. These communities are submerged in a social and cultural introversion that favours the persistence of tribal law and hinders evolution or any change in these damaging customs.[11] Most of the country's Kurdish population is found in the southeast, and is considered by some to be the only ethnic group to commit honour killings. This is not the case, although it is true that, in Turkey, these crimes are more common among this repressed minority. Kurdish women are, then, victims of a double discrimination: not only because of their gender, but also because they belong to this historically persecuted ethnic group.

Associations such as KAMER, founded in 1997, battle every day to change the mentality in these regions, aiming to raise awareness of all involved in these barbaric customs. Their most significant contribution is an emergency team that comes into action when a woman's life is at risk. The group's first task is to search out a mediator responsible for negotiating with the family council to dissuade them, seeking a better alternative than murder. Not any intermediary will do, however. The team investigate the profile of the family they are dealing with to discover whether they are religious, if they speak Turkish, Kurdish, or another language, and their political leanings. Any detail which can help to identify the most appropriate mediator. Members of government, politicians, or imams may all take on this role, as long as they share the same first language as the aggrieved family so as avoid any misunderstanding whatsoever with the offended party. It is important to understand perfectly the customs in that particular area, whether it is a village or town, and endeavour to find a solution that is realistically achievable for this clan. The conciliator meets with the family council and it is in his hands to try change the sentence and, even more importantly, the woman's life.[12]

9

Kill Me Now, If You're a Man!

Zelal did not go to France but ended up hiding in a small town near Istanbul with the family of Emine, her protector. Yet her saviour turned out to be her jailor. The man who had promised her a better life behaved in the same way as the husband from whom she had fled.

Her freedom lasted a matter of seconds, then it was back to the same old story, only with different fists meting out the punches. Beatings once again, even more aggressive when alcohol was involved. Violence sparked by having forgotten to recharge the mobile or any other banal justification. Once more, condemned to another man. The story that repeated itself was eating her up inside.

"Look who wanted to be a self-sufficient woman," she said to herself time and again, the searing pain of those blows that tasted of the past, of defeat. Once more, her rights were violated while he penetrated her, while he confiscated the money she had earned, while he threatened to turn her in to the men who were on her trail.

It was more of the same, though it was harder to swallow. The mistake was all the more painful for having been made a second time; just when Zelal thought she had recovered, she fell back into the same situation, if anything, even worse. The courage that had grown inside her, based on hope for the future, was swept away at a single stroke, bringing her up short against an unchanging reality that, irremediable, could only get worse.

He would hit her hard and then with the same hand that had committed the offence, swear on the Qur'an that no pain had been caused. "She did it herself," Emine repeated over and over, as if all his sins could be wiped clean by denying them. "God is great!" Zelal was a slave once more, though now in the hands of a different thug and for purely sexual motives.

For a year and a half she had felt safe, despite Emine's threats to give her away. An unreal, false situation because her ex-husband's family had not ceased in their search, the objective of cleansing one's honour well worth the investment of resources, time, and effort. Dignity knows not of deadlines or geographical distance; it does not forgive or forget.

From her supposed new home in France, Zelal spoke regularly with her stepmother, who passed on that Mehmet had been calling incessantly, advising them that she was in Turkey, not in Europe as claimed. Where he got this information only the mafias know, but the tip-off made Zelal increasingly uneasy, fearing above all that her own family might discover the deception.

That illusion of safety, marred by the abuse and threats from Emine, evaporated fifteen days ago. A long two weeks since her past once again burst onto the scene, sowing fear and chaos. Fifteen wretched days during which her existence has been a continuous torment; she was frightened to walk, to go outside, to open the door, or to look over her shoulder because her last breath could be just around the next corner.

They came to remind her, to prepare her; her ex-husband only has seven months left to serve in prison and when he gets out, he wants his wife—because she was still his wife—to be waiting at home with the children. Zelal saw them coming, just like the last time in her village. Two familiar faces heading towards her while in her hand, fresh notes just withdrawn from the cash machine. She blinked, opened and closed her eyes in the belief that her mind was playing a trick. "I'm imagining it. I must be," she tried to convince herself. On the verge of passing out, her legs began to tremble and her whole body started to shake.

Those two faces, once again obtruding on her life after a year and a half of silence. What had at first seemed like a cruel figment of her imagination was now becoming more and more tangible. In tears, she phoned Emine and told him that those two spectres of her past were approaching, inescapably.

"You must be mistaken," she heard from the other end of the line.

It was impossible for Zelal to keep her feet, so she decided to sit down on a bench next to a lad who was selling tickets for some show. Her mind was not functioning well enough to remember what they were for.

"Do you feel all right?" asked the young man, concerned.

"It can't be, it can't be," Zelal lamented.

"You're very pale. Would you like me to call an ambulance?"

"No, no, don't worry." She stood up. They were gradually getting closer, each step towards her revealing another feature of those two faces, which were becoming more and more dangerous.

Her body craved nicotine so, despite her panic, Zelal headed towards a cigarette stall a hundred metres away. She felt an urgent need to inhale smoke to calm herself down. Suddenly, a change of heart and, in a replay of a previous escape, the race was on. Running, dodging stalls and street sellers with corn-on-the-cob and *simit*, cutting down side streets, finally reaching the cafe that had been her workplace for the past year. Once again, she had managed to shake them off.

Panic played her a charitable hand, and Zelal was able to explain the situation to her two colleagues. Filled with courage, they set off in search of that man in the peculiar white trousers and green jumper, along with the other, whose outfit was somewhat less outlandish. Luck was not on their side.

A fugitive, Zelal walked home quickly, fearful of every corner, terrified by every shadow. She opened the door to her house, speculating as to who might be inside. Leaving it ajar in case a hasty exit was required, and with her heart beating so hard that it resounded in her throat, she went in. The lights were still turned off. Silently, she crept towards the kitchen, then the living room, and finally a bedroom, where someone was waiting for her. Her whole body trembled once again before recognising the face of that man as her second abuser's father. Emine was out of town but his family, who she hated, was still there. For once, she was glad.

The next day, determination and the need to put an end to this situation overcame prudence and fear. She went looking for them, having first made a few calls. They were not difficult to find.

"We have to talk," said her brother-in-law, the younger of the two, who had just come out of prison.

"I know." It was the only reply that occurred to her.

They went to a regular kind of cafe, for a meeting that was anything but ordinary.

"What do you want from me? How did you find me?"

"You're as stupid as usual. Did you really think you wouldn't leave a single clue? Everybody leaves traces. The telephone company did the job for us. You didn't cancel the line in Istanbul, and they searched for you until they found your new residence and all your documentation in the town hall here," the older brother, with a dark complexion and aggressive eyes, replied disdainfully. She had fed him too, more times than she cared to remember. "So this is where you've been all along, you bitch. We knew that the whole thing about France was a trick," he snapped.

"No, no. I've come here for a meeting, and I'm leaving again in a couple of days."

"Don't lie, bitch. In that case, why is all your documentation here?" They were carrying shotguns at their sides, of course. This most dissuasive of measures was just visible under their jackets each time they moved.

"Well, because I have to keep it somewhere, and I come here to do a lot of interviews. Call the hotel if you want and ask them," said Zelal, mustering confidence in herself where there was none.

"I don't believe you, bitch," he said, never failing to end his remarks with the same cruel epithet.

"Well, take my phone and call the hotel where I'm staying. They'll confirm it for you." It was the very same call that Zelal had made that morning before meeting up with this vile pair. Her friends owned the hotel. She had a good relationship with them, and they had agreed to provide a cover.

"Yes, she checked in yesterday and she is due to leave in two days' time," they answered. The man then hung up.

"You know what we want. Come home to wait for your husband and we'll leave you in peace." There was a clear threat in these words.

"I won't go back." Before their eyes appeared a completely different woman to the one they had known. This was not the submissive Zelal, the same woman who ate the leftovers from their plates, who sat on the floor. And there was even more to come.

"We're not leaving without you, bitch."

The past year and a half disappeared from her mind, replaced by a strength that she never imagined herself to possess. "No, no. I won't go. And watch out, because if I call my friends in the police you'll be back in jail. And this time for twenty years."

"Do as you're told, woman!" There was contempt, anger, fear, and rage in those words.

"No! Kill me now if you're a man!" The words flew out of her mouth like poisoned darts, uncontrolled. "If you're men, then kill me! Come on! Do it!"

"You know that we haven't received the order. Otherwise we wouldn't be here talking."

She did not know. Could it be that her husband had changed his mind and that he wanted her at his side? Or perhaps the only thing he sought was the pleasure of killing her himself when he got out of jail. She had no idea, but without an order, without the agreement of the family council, these puppets of the clan could not do a thing. Courage swelled within her.

"Kill me and if not, then leave, because I'll call the police right now."

"You'll die any day now. Any day, bitch." There was not a hint of doubt in her brother-in-law's words.

"They didn't do shit. They left," snaps Zelal in an insulting rash of fury. The auburn-haired woman now spits out her story with the harshest, most acid tone that she has used to this point. She is no longer crying and seems strong, tough, untouchable, and superior. But then the other Zelal appears, the woman who is forced to flee, who has been hiding out since that day in an apartment belonging to some relatives of her partner in Istanbul. The woman who endures beatings from Emine, a man who humiliates her every day yet appears to be her only salvation.

She has to flee the country, to leave him. Next time, there will be an order from the family council or it will be her own ex-husband who comes to kill her. What difference does it make? It doesn't matter who does it! She will be dead. And the worst thing is that if she cannot prove to her family that she is living in France, it will be her own stepbrother who puts an end to her life.

She cries, although she learnt not to because it achieves nothing. She cries because her only salvation now is a visa. She smokes, inhaling from every cigarette as though each drag could rid her of some of the filth inside or kill her a little more, she doesn't care. Countless tears emerge from those round, brown eyes and she breathes in the cigarette smoke as if she were breathing in life itself, sucking it dry in case it vanishes, in case this turns out to be her last moment.

10

On Laws and Raising Awareness

Zelal's only consolation, if it can be called that, is the knowledge that her killers will not go unpunished, like so many others who benefitted from the old Turkish penal code and from sexist judges who applied the law according to their own convictions.

What could be expected of legislation that considered a woman's body and sexuality to be the property of her family, her husband, and society? Everyone's property except her own. In line with this concept, rape was an offence against these three possible owners, never against the individual, that is to say, never against the woman who, at the end of the day, had been abused.

Women were not permitted the luxury of considering themselves victims because the aggrieved were the men who owned them. An example of this is the fact that if a woman was raped or kidnapped, her abuser would not be condemned if he later married her, as in this way the family's honour would supposedly be restored.[13]

The enormous effort on the part of women's organisations ensured that the new civil and penal codes approved in Turkey in 2002 and 2005 respectively were, at least on paper, equalitarian and abolished gender differences. Thanks to the new Turkish laws, it is no longer permissible to use provocation as an excuse to reduce sentences, as occurred in the past with honour crimes, and adults who force minors to commit violent crimes are considered legally responsible for that murder.

However, there are still gaps in the legislation, used by the perpetrators of these crimes and by witnesses when they appear in court. Despite the bold efforts of feminist groups, the penal code does not consider honour crime as an aggravating factor requiring the maximum sentence, so leaving plenty of leeway for a whole range of tactics on the part of defence lawyers.

To the killers' further benefit is the fact that justice is still administered by a judicial system educated in this very same patriarchal, sexist society. It has been these judges who, in many cases, have given biased verdicts favouring the murderers. It must be taken into account that many of them were born and brought up in the southeast and find it difficult to view as illegitimate crimes committed in the name of honour, which they still consider a fundamental principle.[14] It is a problem of mentality, which still persists in Turkish society, even among educated groups and in spite of the law. However, women's organisations and the media are trying to develop public awareness and pressure magistrates to ensure that it is no longer heroes who emerge from their courtrooms, but convicts.

Without a doubt, perpetrators are being left with less and less room to manoeuvre and judges are now applying sentences that set an example so that residents of the most traditional Anatolia come to view these murders as real crimes with serious legal consequences.

11

Why? Why? Why Me?

"Why? Why is this happening to me and not to you women? Why?" An awkward silence follows and then comes the answer.

"Because you were born in the wrong place." This is the clear and crushing reality according to the Turkish woman who is today sitting opposite Zelal and whose life is so far removed from hers.

Zelal remains silent for four minutes before all the feelings bottled up inside come spilling out.

"I'll tell you why. Because they're ignorant and uneducated. Because they're not human beings. Because they don't know what they have in their hands. Or maybe just because they're men. Because they don't know how to look after a woman. Because they view women as a commodity. Because they grow up seeing how their fathers treat their mothers and they think that's just the way it is. Because they don't think about anything. Because they believe that only what they say is true." She breaks down in tears, struggling to pull herself together by means of cigarettes and more cigarettes. She goes on. "And now, what am I? A prostitute. What difference is there between me and those women?" Silence once again, then a long, exhausting drag on her cigarette and she answers out loud, "That I only do it with one man. Why? Why? Why me? They've been killing me little by little since the day I was born. They wouldn't let me go to university because moving to another city alone is for whores. And look what I've become. If I'd been born in a different family, I'd be a doctor now." Her brown eyes are flooded with tears but the torrent of words is uninterrupted. "I've never, ever done what I wanted in life. Why? Because they didn't let me do anything. And now I've got no money and no work. Do you know what? I haven't got a single lira because they've taken everything from me and I have to live with this man who abuses me. The only solution is to work, to find a job, but now it has to be abroad, in another country, because if my family find out they'll kill me. If they discover that I've lied to them they'll slit my throat. And me...what can I do without them? What can I do if I'm dead? I need to live."

It is a barrage of ideas, mental connections, comings and goings; of words, phrases, and pained expressions slowed down only by long drags at her cigarette. She inhales the smoke as if the world depended on it, then picks up the pace once again. "That's right. There's no solution. I can't go to a women's organisation because they can't help me. What can they do for me? You tell me—what can they do for me? Let me stay in a refuge for four months and then...what? Throw me out onto the street again, without a job. And me...how can I live? What can I do? They don't have economic resources and they can't get me a job....If that's my choice, I'd rather stay as I am, with this cursed man. I'm not going to an organisation if they don't promise me a job." Her words are a mass of ideas that sometimes contradict themselves. "If I'm with a man for his money I'll be a prisoner again. What's more, I don't want any more sex in my whole life. It's disgusting. I don't want anyone to touch me. I hate all the men that look at me when I walk down the street, they're all the same." She rests, then continues without being asked a single question. "The only thing I have is this," pointing to a white-gold diamond ring, which does not appear to be of very good quality. "This is all I have. I don't have anything in the bank, I don't have a house, I don't have any money. He kept it all. I have absolutely nothing. And, on top of that, I can't stay in my country because they want to kill me. Can you tell me what I can do?"

There is no reply.

"Can anyone tell me what I can do?"

Women's organisations try to provide shelter for these desperate women, hiding them in secret refuges scattered around Istanbul. Zelal, however, does not trust them. Not even the police know her whereabouts because the security forces in Turkey are not always to be trusted and, more often than one would hope, end up revealing women's hideouts to their families in exchange for substantial bribes. The clans are too powerful, to such a point that, if a woman is being pursued by too many people, the refuges refuse to take her in, fearing that they will end up blowing the covers of all the other residents or that there will be a shoot out in their facilities. It would not be the first time that something like this has happened.

Be that as it may, these organisations continue to be the only means of escape for many "undesirables," though they do not always manage to get back on their feet. In these centres, women receive psychological care along with basic training and IT knowledge, which will help them to carve out a future for themselves. There, they find support and understanding, sharing a roof with other women who have lived through the same experiences, who identify with their stories and empathise with their feelings.

Yet there are few and resources are scarce. The main problem in this country is the lack of women's centres. If, legally, there should be 1,400 refuges in Turkey, the reality is that there are only 30 centres in the whole country to serve a female population of over 35 million.[15] At the present time, it seems that this situation is set to continue as neither the government nor the opposition parties are inclined to invest time, effort, or money in improving existing facilities or creating new ones. There is, in effect, no real political will to bring about change, and comments such as, "If we open more centres, they'll turn into brothels," illustrate the sexist response to a problem that seems to concern only women and not society as a whole.

12

The Coffee Grounds that Say Nothing

Zelal is unable to read her future in the grounds of her thick Turkish coffee. They tell her nothing of what lies ahead. They are elusive and evasive, when they have always been clear to her. This clairvoyance, which she turned into a business, predicting what tomorrow would bring for her clients, does not work when it comes to her own flesh and bones. The grounds say nothing of her person. They give no signs, no indications of what is to come. But she does know hundreds of stories about Kurdish women that have tragic endings. Too many. Will her story finish in the same way?

In a suburb on the outskirts of Istanbul she says good-bye, tired and nervous, always looking behind in case anyone is following her. She leaves us with uncertainty and the promise of a call to advise us of any change in her circumstances.

The telephone rings and the tears of the old, weak Zelal flood the line. She was not given a visa. She will return to her village. With her people. There she was born, and there she will die.

Part 2

The Pious

And tell believing women that they should lower their glances, guard their private parts, and not display their charms beyond what [it is acceptable] to reveal; they should let their headscarves fall to cover their necklines and not reveal their charms except to their husbands, their fathers, their husbands' fathers, their sons, their husbands' sons, their brothers, their brothers' sons, their sisters' sons, their womenfolk, their slaves, such men as attend them who have no sexual desire, or children who are not yet aware of women's nakedness; they should not stamp their feet so as to draw attention to any hidden charms.

The Qur'an, 24:31 from *Oxford World's Classics* (2004), translated by M.A.S. Abdel Haleem

13

Superman's Phone Booth

Sennur jokes about her appearance, as she does whenever she is at the university. "Have you seen the way they make me dress?" she asks, pointing to the small white beach hat pulled down tight on top of her Islamic headscarf in an effort to cover it up. It is not the least bit hidden. In fact, it can be clearly discerned from all angles. It is blindingly obvious, like those worn by many of Sennur's classmates at the prestigious Bosphorus University in Istanbul. There, girls search out ways to keep within the Turkish law banning the hijab in education centres yet at the same time avoid contravening their religious beliefs.

"That's where they make us get changed. It's Superman's phone booth," explains Sennur ironically, gesturing to a kind of green call box at the entrance to the university facilities. It seems like a building-site cabin where workers might get changed at the start of the day or a portaloo for some large-scale event. In that booth, the daily transformation of this particular heroine takes place. Every morning, Sennur and her friends repeat the same process: cover their heads, already covered by a headscarf also known as a *türban*, but this time with a hat.

The procedure is bothersome and repetitive, but at this university, where Turkish legislation is interpreted in a more lax, permissive way, it is effective. Elsewhere, the hat trick does not work and it is necessary to resort to strategies even more imaginative, like wearing a wig.

Outside, the attentive gaze of security guards stationed at the entrance post traces yet another threshold for these girls' freedom of dress. From the changing booth onwards, across the extensive facilities of this former American college one can see long-haired girls sporting the latest European fashions, with jeans and fitted T-shirts and others, like Sennur, who hide their bodies beneath full-length coats and headscarves topped off with outlandish hats.

"It's so unfair! It really hurts that they don't let me live and dress according to my beliefs," Sennur confesses. Because this young woman, at twenty-three, is chatty, bright, and outgoing, bursting with desire to shout to the four winds that she considers herself modern and that her hijab is not a symbol of ignorance or lack of education as many in Turkey believe. Sennur does not understand it. However much she tries, it is impossible to grasp why, in her country, where the immense majority of the population is Muslim, she and all the other women who use the Islamic headscarf are not allowed into university. What is more, she is unable to comprehend why it is also against the law to use a headscarf in government workplaces, military headquarters, parliament, and even in courts of law if the woman in question is a lawyer. "This doesn't even happen in Europe, despite Muslims not being the majority there," she ponders out loud.

However, this has been the reality in Turkey since the end of the eighties when it was determined that wearing a headscarf undermined the Republic's nonreligious principles.[1]

The Euro-Asian giant is a secular state governed according to the laws approved by the idolised leader, Mustafá Kemal Atatürk, who founded the Republic in 1923. There is no place here for liberties of a kind that hark back to the religious values of the extinct Ottoman Empire. It is of no importance that the majority still consider

---

[1] The Turkish Constitutional Court ruled in 1989 to annul a reform of the education laws put forward by the centre-right Motherland Party in 1988, considering it a breach of the country's secular principles.

themselves Muslim or that 60 percent of women cover their heads.[1] In this young nation, created by the visionary Atatürk, sultans and caliphates are a thing of the past and Islam should be relegated to the private sphere.

And so it occurs that the headscarf, the hijab, is the major bone of contention in modern-day Turkish society. A question upon which the country's population is increasingly divided: a nation polarized, most of all among its elite, split in two by opposing ideals. The so-called moderate Islamists, headed by Prime Minister Recep Tayyip Erdogan, opt for a lifestyle influenced by religious precepts and consider the ban an "injustice." The Kemalists meanwhile, led by the army, judges, and opposition, view the use of a headscarf as a symbol of politicised Islam, which will end up turning Turkey into a country ruled by *Sharia* (Islamic law), destroying the basic principles of the secular constitution.[2]

"They think that those of us who wear headscarves are a danger for Turkey but they should realise that's not the case. We're not going to force everyone else to put one on," Sennur would say to anyone with a mind to listen.

This devout young woman fails to understand why her freedom of dress is limited and why girls with European attitudes look down on her, viewing her hijab as a symbol of religious fanaticism and oppression that must be eradicated. "I'm not oppressed in the least," she says. "And if they think I'm stupid and forced to wear it, then they're wrong."

Sennur strolls around the lush gardens at Bosphorus University in her hat, feeling discriminated against for her beliefs, struggling to ensure that the security guards on their rounds never spot her

---

[1] 63% of the female population cover their heads, according to a study carried out by the Turkish Economic and Social Studies Foundation (TESEV). In their book, *Religion, Society and Politics in a Changing Turkey*, published in August 2007, the sociologists Binnaz Toprak and Ali Çarkoglu point out that 48.8% of women use a traditional scarf, while 11.4% wear an Islamic veil or *türban*. Just 1.1% opt for the *çarçaf*, which only leaves the eyes uncovered.

[2] It is not only an ideological battle, but a power struggle between the country's old oligarchy, with their European-style education, urban outlook and secular values, and the traditional, pious usurpers of this previously undisputed authority: members of the governing Justice and Development Part (AKP).

without the cap. That could cost a warning or even result in her being expelled from the university.

"If you wear a headscarf they think you can't be modern, you're not getting an education and you're ignorant. But it's not like that. I'm a university student and I know what's going on in the world. I'm not old-fashioned, stuck in the past. I'm modern. The ones who really have a closed mind are people who think that kind of thing about us," she claims, visibly upset.

14

Islam, Televisions, and Gems

Since childhood, when she would repeat verses from the Qur'an with her mother over the kitchen stove, Islam has guided Sennur's lifestyle and clothing. In her hometown of Kutahya, a city in central Anatolia, she attended mixed summer courses given at the village mosque, where the imam taught the doctrine passed on by Mohammed through the sacred book.

Since then, her alarm clock has gone off every morning at five o'clock and Sennur gets ups to perform the ritual washing before prayer. Her small hands come first then she rinses her mouth, with its plump lips and immaculate teeth, and cleans her snub nose, her two hazel eyes watching over. Her pale, rounded face is splashed with water then she scrubs her long forearms and wets the top of her head before cleaning out and washing behind her ears. To finish, she washes her elegant neck and slim, bony feet. Afterwards, she puts on a *türban*, leaving only her face uncovered, and in the tiny living room of her neat student flat, on a little rug with Persian motifs in shades of brown, she sets about the ritual genuflecting typical of Muslim prayer.

Her svelte, well-proportioned form—although it is difficult to make out her figure clearly beneath the loose smock she is wearing—moves in an agile, rhythmic way while she thanks Allah for everything she has, then greets the good angel on her right and bad angel on her left. With a shy but clear voice, Sennur murmurs passages from the Qur'an, repeating them four times before returning to the arms of Morpheus.

The muezzin will call her to prayer on four other occasions during the day, from the countless minarets scattered across the city where she now lives: Istanbul, the ancient capital of the Ottoman Empire. Wherever she happens to be, Sennur will search out a place to pray before hearing the next cry of "Allah is great! There is no God but Allah, and Mohammed is his prophet." She would not feel comfortable ignoring this call, as it is prayer, which gives her the most satisfaction each day.

"When I pray, I realise that I'm not alone. God is there. It's a moment to break off from life and reflect, relax. And to organise my time, too."

The university does not have a mosque where students can perform their ritual washing and prayers. Turkey is a secular country and that would be unthinkable. So, after hearing the *ezan*, Sennur waits nervously for the next break between classes, then runs like a soul possessed to the residence halls in the centre of the campus and charges up the stairs to the room of her most devout friends. She whips off the extravagant hat covering her veil and quickly washes those parts of her body that may have got dirty since the last prayers. There, in a small room with four beds, she begins her midday conversation with Allah. The precise series of gestures and genuflections are now repeated ten times then it is another race back to the classroom to continue with her studies.

If she is in the street, she will look for a mosque in which to pray. If out shopping, then one of the mall's designated prayer rooms will be her chosen venue. When travelling inside Turkey, petrol stations become her temporary places of worship. Yet the time Sennur feels closest to God is when she communicates with Him from the mountains, only the sky above her, always facing Mecca.

"The only thing I have to do is find a place where there are no men, because with these movements we make, bending over, it wouldn't be good if they saw us," she explains. It is for this reason, because of men, to hide herself from them, that she covers her head. Not as a symbol of political Islam. Sennur holds these beliefs so firm that she finds it deeply offensive for anyone to dismiss her decision as partisan, her only objective being to follow God's commandments.

"Allah is always thinking and finding solutions for problems we might have, even before they arise. He knows everything. He understands me and sees the danger that men might pose for me. When he revealed the book to the prophet, he knew it. That's why he let it be known that I should wear a veil and hide myself from men's gaze. I don't question his commands; I obey them." Just in case her idea has not come across clearly, Sennur gives an example; it is a common feature of the way she expresses herself. "It's as if I were a television. Who knows best how it works? The one who made it and designed the instruction manual. Allah created that manual, which is the Qur'an; it has never changed and never will. He knows me better than my mother and is perfectly clear about what's best for me," she says, with profound conviction.

This line of thinking is what led Sennur, at eleven, to put on a hijab for the first time. She states that it was a freely taken decision, without any coercion from her parents or any other relative, and insists that her only aim was to follow God's commandments and protect herself from the threats of the outside world. Even more so, taking into account that—according to what she has studied in the sacred book—Sennur considers herself a gem, a precious stone to be protected and kept safe from people's view. Covered. "When Mohammed came across a man pulling hard on the reins of his camel, he said 'Take care of the jewel you are carrying.' He was referring to the woman sitting behind him. We are gems reserved for our husbands," she explains enthusiastically.

This young woman questions nothing that is written in the Qur'an. It never even crosses her mind to regard the headscarf as a means of controlling or degrading women. "Allah is kind and permissive with us. In fact, the rules we must follow during our period are made by the angels as we're exempt from genuflecting or bearing the weight of the holy book. God is conscious that we're weak during those days and that's why his commandments are more flexible." It does not occur to her that she might be considered impure and unfit to touch the sacred writings, as some in the West affirm. "For him, we are very important. In fact, that's why a whole chapter of the Qur'an is dedicated to us," she asserts.

As much as she insists on explaining that the *türban* is not a political symbol, this very idea causes nightmares for many in secular Turkey; they believe that the headscarf, not the light bulb, is the true emblem of the governing Justice and Development Party (AKP).

As further evidence that there is no hidden political agenda behind her use of the hijab, Sennur argues that she also follows to the letter every other rule on dress laid down by her religion. She always wears a *pardesü* (a long coat that makes it impossible to discern her figure) together with an ankle-length skirt, which she would never swap for trousers. Tights in summer and Islamic headscarf. Everything in perfectly coordinated shades, of course. A green scarf with a beige pattern by Pierre Cardin, worn with a light camel blouse and matching skirt with an emerald line forming large checks. She wears white tights, shoes the same colour as her clothes, and an immaculate fabric handbag decorated with a huge flower.

She does not use makeup, earrings or other accessories, but has eyebrows shaped with almost mathematical precision and takes the greatest care with every single detail of her outfit. "I want to look beautiful. I'm a woman and I like to feel attractive, but religion comes first," she confesses. Sennur loves to buy herself pretty clothes, especially shoes, and treats herself to a new pair as often as possible. Whenever her tight university schedule permits, she heads off to Cevahir, a mall in central Istanbul, and spends the day shopping. Her friends laugh when she comes home weighed down with bags.

15

The Nightmare

The first day Sennur crossed the doorway of the Imam Hatip religious school, it was with a veil covering her head. That was the first time she put one on. She was eleven and although not a full-fledged young woman, as her periods had yet to start, the school's dress code for girls was very clear.

It was 1996 and the Islamic headscarf had already been censured for some time in primary classrooms and universities, despite the continuous efforts of the political party then in government to bring an end to its forced absence. However, the Islamic school that Sennur would attend was a special institution for educating children who would go on to be imams at mosques. There, the *türban* was not prohibited; on the contrary, its use was obligatory.

At this centre, the curriculum combined exhaustive study of the Qur'an with training in science and letters. And so she learnt Arabic, studied the roots of her religion, and memorised every word of the Holy Book. She was and still is able to read the Qur'an as few Turks can, in its original language and understands what is written. Most of her fellow countrymen recite it without knowing what it means.

But then, with Sennur in her second year at the school, Turkey suffered a military coup.[1] The outcome was that all laws aimed at safeguarding the Republic's secular principles were strengthened and enforced. These included tough controls on universities, where no one wearing an Islamic headscarf has been able to enter since that time without being reprimanded or expelled. Access to a university education was also hindered for students from the Iman Hatip school due to fears that the school might serve as an entrance point through which Islamists could move into the upper ranks of public administration, and as a result, hold key posts in government. Faced with this situation, Sennur's teachers encouraged their outstanding young student to change schools; otherwise, her professional future would be cut short. It was then that she decided to begin her studies at Kutahya School for Teachers, despite the *türban* being strictly prohibited.

At that time, when she was fourteen, Sennur had her first period; a day when she paid more attention than ever before to the important task of covering not only her head but also her body. Trousers and short-sleeved shirts were gone forever. This step, from being a girl to becoming a woman, required a greater commitment to God and a stricter compliance with his commandments. She was no longer a silly, runny-nosed kid. So when she took off her headscarf at the entrance to her new school, it felt like she had died. "It was horrible. With that action, I was consciously going against everything I believed in. Until then, I was just a child. I felt that I was betraying myself and Allah too, that nothing could possibly be worse," she recalls. But she was mistaken.

The days passed by, and little by little she got used to the new morning ritual of unveiling her head beneath the huge entranceway of the girls' school in Kutahya. Every morning, in the school's sterile, neglected garden, the headmaster would assemble his pupils in perfectly straight lines and wish them good day. Afterwards, one by one and in alphabetical order, as called out by their teachers, the

---

[1] The armed forces obliged the government to step down in 1997 in what is now known as a postmodern coup. Certain policies on religious issues from Necmettin Erbakan's government were viewed by the military as dangerous for the Republic so they issued an ultimatum to Erbakan, insisting that he resign, and he bowed out.

girls were submitted to the very strictest inspection of their clothing. School medal around their neck, uniform ironed, skirt at just the right length, and long, flowing locks.

Only one teacher there covered her hair. Sennur used to bump into her at the entrance each morning; just like her students, she was obliged to scrupulously follow the rules imposed by a state that views a European style of dress as the role model for modernity. The *türban*, however, did not yet determine students' results. You, with a veil: seven marks. You, without one: ten marks. That was to come later.

Not even in her worst nightmares did Sennur imagine what was to occur on May 19, 1999. Every year, Turkey celebrates this special day honouring young people, set up at the express wish of Atatürk. It is a national holiday when all schools in the country, without exception, organise festivities for children. It is a time to honour the Republic's founder but also to have fun.

Preparations for this long-awaited event got underway months in advance, and the girls eagerly rehearsed their parts for different theatre productions as well as their dance steps. Days of repetition upon repetition. There were plenty of nerves and, as always, wonderful sets decorating Kutahya's largest stadium. The big day approached, with fifty different schools all working to prepare their performances. Sennur knew by heart each movement of the choreography she had rehearsed so many times, both at home and at school. The dance was replete with pirouettes and little jumps and would culminate when she and her classmates deposited large baskets of flowers in the centre of the stadium.

"This is the outfit you'll wear for the show," the teacher said to them.

She could not believe her eyes. She was speechless. The sight of that tiny red miniskirt with matching sleeveless top left her paralysed. Sennur could do nothing to avoid it, and her parents were aware of this too. For days, it was impossible to sleep as she turned over in her mind that moment which was, irremediably, upon her. She felt powerless.

The dreaded occasion arrived and she had no choice but to put on the costume and take the stage. To dance, dressed like that, before hundreds of people. While she moved around the stadium, which was packed out with men, in that minuscule skirt and without her headscarf, Sennur thought of Allah and asked forgiveness for breaking her promise. "I'm sorry, Lord. I'm sorry, Lord. I'm sorry, I'm sorry, I'm sorry...what can I do? I'm sorry, I'm sorry," she repeated, over and over again. Carried along by inertia, concentrating on her thoughts more than her dance steps, she alternated phrases from the Qur'an with these apologies. "How can this be happening to me?" she asked herself, leaning over to lay her basket of flowers on the ground, the miniskirt now revealing even more centimetres of her body.

Her eyes wandered to the spot where her mother was sitting. A headscarf covered her hair but she felt no better than Sennur. It hurt to see her daughter like this.

For the second time, Sennur's whole body agonized with the pain of living in a country where it is prohibited to use what, for this young woman, is the principal symbol of her submission to God.

To avoid living through such a bitter experience again, Sennur took the preventive measure of joining the school band for the next year. It was the only option that occurred to her as a way of performing at the event in a skirt long enough to cover her knees. The musicians' uniforms had always been perfectly modest and there was no reason for this to change.

16

To University, in a Headscarf

The daughter of a coal company worker and a housewife, Sennur was always certain that she did not want to stay in Kutahya. Her life would be different than that of her mother, always confined within the four walls of the house, relegated to the cooking and cleaning. She did not want her existence limited to the women's get-togethers in friends' homes; conversations where, from start to finish, mothers-in-law or daughters-in-law are pulled to pieces, the national sport among Turkish women. Exchanging opinions on the latest television soaps, in which arguments between mothers and their sons' wives are the common denominator, was not an activity that this young woman aspired to.

She would go to whichever university offered her a place to become a math teacher, even though this might mean studying for her degree without using the hijab. That said, the first place on her list of preferences was reserved for Bosphorus University, considered to be among the most permissive in its dress policy for women students, along with the private college, Bilgi.

Rumours abound among devout Turkish women, and all of them are up to date on which centres are more flexible or, like Istanbul University, have not admitted a single person wearing a headscarf since the coup in 1997. Many students and teachers there have been expelled, officially reprimanded, or cautioned. So strictly is the legislation enforced at this university that even photos of past students wearing headscarves were banned from an anniversary commemoration album that was supposed to include all alumni that had graduated since the centre first opened. The faces of those graduates, who had finished their studies prior to 1996, having suffered no discrimination whatsoever, would be mercilessly censured years later.

Yet in the end, Sennur managed to secure a place at Bosphorus University, Turkey's most prestigious centre and also the toughest to access. Excellent grades and an outstanding entrance exam backed up her application.

So there she was, in Istanbul; a city with hundreds of mosques and a cosmopolitan, European air. It was the "great ocean" where she must now swim, after splashing around in the "pool" that was Kuthaya. From the very first instant she set foot in the place, once the ancient city of Byzantium, Sennur was caught in its spell, despite the fact that the hateful ritual she nicknamed "Superman's phone booth" would begin here. Far from turning her into a superhero, it makes her feel degraded, that ridiculous hat branding her as inferior.

The positive side of this diabolical routine was that, once outside the cubicle, not a single classmate viewed her extravagant outfit with the least contempt. Yet her lectures were attended by a mix of students from other countries along with Turkish girls, not religious in the least, who wore the latest European fashions, the shortest of skirts, and plenty of makeup. No one forgets the centre's principles, which advocate progress, tolerance, and freedom. Well, not quite everyone. Certain teachers are not so open minded, despite the laudable ethic postulated by the faculty.

In her first year, Sennur decided, along with one of her "pious" friends, to join an advanced English-language course at the university. She had heard about one particular teacher with a reputation for making even the least talented students speak the language of Shakespeare. So, without giving it further thought, Sennur decided to register.

"Please look for another class," said the teacher.

"What do you mean?" asked Sennur.

"Just what you heard. Register for an online English course or look for another tutor," answered the English-language expert, without the least misgiving.

That was the first time she clashed with a university lecturer, but it would not be the last. Although the professors claim to be liberal, some of them even educated in Europe, according to Sennur they are not impartial when it comes to evaluating their students, issues such as the *türban* being taken into account when awarding grades.

During those first years at the University, the Justice and Development Party was already in power. Though they would have willingly pushed forward with policies to lift the veto on the hijab—above all, because most of the party leaders' wives wore a headscarf—they did not do so for fear of a reaction from the army. As self-appointed guardians of the secular state, Turkey's military leaders are prone to venture well beyond their barracks whenever they see it in danger.

In the second year of her degree courses, Sennur opened the newspaper and read a ruling from the European Commission on Human Rights. Her heart sank. "Not even the Europeans defend us on this issue!" she complains.

Leyla Sahin, a medical student, had brought a case against Turkey in the European Court of Human Rights, claiming that her fundamental right to education had been infringed. In 1998, during her fifth year at Istanbul University, the Vice-Chancellor issued a decree informing students that anyone with an Islamic headscarf would be refused admission to classes, courses, and tutorials. As a result, Leyla was unable to sit for exams in a number of subjects, register for courses, or attend lectures.

The ruling issued by the European institution was emphatic and deeply discouraging for women like Sennur: "There has been no violation of the freedom of thought, conscience, or religion," nor any unjustified interference with her right to education.

In her third year at university, Sennur again opened the newspaper and, this time, was staggered to read that the country's then president, a convinced Kemalist,[1] had refused to invite the wives of

[1] Ahmet Necdet Sezer was President of the Republic from May 2000 until 2007, when Abdullah Gül was elected.

all the leading government ministers to a reception at the presidential palace because they wore headscarves. Even the wife of Prime Minister Recep Tayyip Erdogan was excluded. All senior government figures should have attended, yet representatives of the party then in power refused to do so as a sign of protest. The atmosphere in Istanbul became increasingly heated, and Sennur felt miserable at having a government unable to do anything to improve the situation.

The worst arrived in May of 2006. When she remembers it, Sennur wishes she could lock herself in the house and cry; cry until someone arrived and told her that it was all a bad dream, that the reality was different, that it was all a nightmare. An Islamic extremist had burst into the Council of State in Ankara, shooting at the judges who ruled to uphold a decision banning a nursery school teacher from wearing a hijab. The outcome was one death and four injured, a black day in Turkey's judicial history.

"That's not the way!" she would shout. "I don't believe there are people who kill for religious reasons. These men are paid by our enemies to make their crimes look like the work of Islamic extremists. But whoever does this is going against what is written in the Qur'an. The Holy Book says we must not kill, we must not attack others," the young woman concludes, furiously.

She was unaware that, years later, her suspicions would be confirmed: an ultra-nationalist group would be accused of perpetrating this murder. It was one violent attack within a much broader plot that aimed to provoke chaos in Turkey and justify a military coup to remove the governing party, the Islamic AKP.[1]

[1] It is known as the Ergenekon Group. A trial against over eighty people began in October 2008 and, according to the public prosecutor, there is enough evidence to implicate this organisation in the judge's murder.

17

Shopping for Wigs

Sennur considers herself lucky at times. Most of all, when she goes shopping with her friends, looking for wigs in the bazaars or along the street by Taksim Square that is lined with stores, one after another, all selling synthetic hair.

Wigs have become a lifesaver for many women. A self-imposed and not particularly flattering fashion, but at the end of the day, an imaginative formula like any other to battle against the strict rules at most universities in Istanbul. There, a simple beach hat is not enough to skirt the laws, which vice-chancellors apply to the letter. So, fake locks serve as headscarves, hiding girls' real hair and complying with the precepts of humility and modesty advocated by Islam.

However, many young women complain that this solution provides no safeguard against discrimination from teachers, who take these hairpieces into account when evaluating students and award them lower grades than their secular classmates. Ashamed of their appearance, these girls claim that the wigs are a kind of stigma, a faculty-wide target of gawping or ridicule. In any case, they would rather have this than go uncovered.

A synthetic hairdo accompanied one of Sennur's friends during her four years at the university. The bathrooms close to Istanbul

University witnessed her daily metamorphosis, in which Superman's phone booth could play no part. The market-stall wig, in a plastic bag, would become her essential study tool. And public toilets would provide the setting for her particular transformation. "It was terrible. Who would want to go out looking like this?" she recalls, hoping never again to live through a similar psychological trauma.

It seems impossible to determine the exact number of women driven out of university as, in many cases, the reason for this forced exile has been a lack of attendance in class. Of course, behind these absences lies the fact that it is impossible to come through the door wearing an Islamic headscarf. Some organisations speak in hundreds of thousands, yet these figures are impossible to corroborate given that there are girls who have not even attempted to access higher education. They had no intention whatsoever of taking off their headscarves.[16]

18

Exile

With sadness, resignation, a tinge of anger and an element of despair, Sennur waved good-bye to her friends as they left Turkey to complete their university studies abroad. They could not bear dressing up in ugly wigs or ridiculous hats and headed to other countries where the law allowed them to attend class in an Islamic headscarf.

"My classmates have fled to Europe and America. I would never have gone. I prefer to stay here, even though the situation bothers me. I won't be forced to leave my country and, even less, give up my education. At the end of the day, that's what these people want. They put all these obstacles in the way so that we can't get a higher education and take their jobs. They'd rather write us off as ignorant; to say that we don't know anything, we're not modern. But I refuse to accept that. I'd rather take off the *türban* because I really believe that university is important. A person can read a lot but, in the end, the training you receive at university is key, it's what counts the most." Sennur has no doubt that she took the right decision.

Other women, however, have decided to withdraw from the struggle played out at the doors of Turkish universities. One of them was Ayse, a medical student. "I'll be back." Those were the words she left written in marker on the wall of the classroom at Hacettepe

University, where she had studied for almost two years. It was the year 2000 and her decision was made: she would go abroad, to Vienna. Ayse could see no other way out of the predicament she faced. As much as her friends insisted, taking off her headscarf was not an option. Nor would she give up the studies that were fundamental for her professional development. She had already experienced the bitter taste of going against her principles, being forced to attend high school without covering her hair, and wasn't prepared to relive the same psychological trauma she was still struggling to overcome. The way she was forced to behave was "schizophrenic." "It felt as if I was one person before going through the door, then a totally different girl once inside," she explains. At least that was her experience and it was impossible to stand this contradiction any longer.

Eight years have passed and, despite those letters written on the wall of that classroom, today packed with women whose heads go uncovered, Ayse has yet to return. It is hard for her to imagine coming back, even more so as a doctor. She may be able to find work in a public hospital because although there are rules against women with a *türban*, people tend to turn a blind eye. However, like many other female doctors, she would have to hide away, become invisible to the eyes of many patients. The thought of a life like this sends a shiver down her spine.

A similar route was taken by the two daughters of Prime Minister Recep Tayyip Erdogan. They too graduated from foreign universities, far from their revered nation, in countries where the majority of the population is not Muslim but religious customs are respected without any detriment to a student's grades.

However, only a limited number of women have emigrated for this reason. It is estimated that just 1 percent opt to abandon their motherland, to back down in the face of legislation which seems unshakeable. For many, a lack of resources is key. But organisations such as AKDER—set up by two students forced to put their studies in Turkey on hold—raise funds to ensure that young women with limited finances can continue their degrees abroad. Grades also play a fundamental role in admitting these girls to European universities. If they are not very good students, they will not be able to go.

In caps, wigs, or by heading abroad, each rides out the headscarves storm in the way that best fits their personality. Others cannot find a way to balance education with their religious principles and so accept defeat. That is just what happened to Suna, a girl Sennur knew. After passing fourth-year exams in medicine and with only two years left to complete, she gave up her studies. For this young woman, it was impossible to find a solution. Taking off her headscarf in public was too painful, and she could not afford to embark on a foreign adventure. So, Suna got married, had two children, and now works, though not as a doctor. Her determination is undimmed, and if the rules change one day, she will return to university. She is in no doubt about that.

Yet there are many more cases that our protagonist has not even heard about. The youthful and cheery Havva, in her colourful hijab, outlandish necklaces, and Converse trainers is a new, more recent example of this prohibition. For the last several years, it has impossible to take the university entrance exam wearing a headscarf. So there she is, at home, waiting for a solution that may never come. This chatty young woman, not yet eighteen, believes that taking off her hijab is "like being forced to unbutton your shirt in public, to get undressed in front of other people." Havva's future could well be limited to the kitchen pans unless she gives way, or Turkey approves a rule that could free her from this dilemma, the same dichotomy in which many women of this country now live.

19

Neither Hugs nor Kisses, Eyes Fixed on the Tiles

When Sennur arrives from university and removes her headscarf, the shadow it cast over her face disappears and her pretty, dark-brown hair comes into view. In the privacy of her home, she also takes off her glasses and *pardesü*, baring a pale, svelte body and revealing a perfectly proportioned, delicate young woman. Her boyfriend, Mehmet, has never seen her so lightly dressed, although they have been going out together for two years. The young man will have to wait until they are married to enjoy her beauty, just as he bides his time in the hope of a simple kiss. So far, any kind of sexual interaction between the couple has been nonexistent. And we are referring to kisses, hugs, or caresses because anything more intimate would be unthinkable.

He is devout, just like her: a follower of the same Islamic principles as his girlfriend. Perhaps even more religious than Sennur, he accepts that his destiny is a long wait. How could one fail to do so and ruin the chance of marrying a diamond intact? At times, his libido betrays him and he seeks physical contact with Sennur, even if it is only a caress. Afterwards come the pangs of remorse, and the young woman's sleepless nights over a fleeting touch do not seem to compensate for having broken the religious rules.

"Forgive me, Lord. It won't happen again. I promise, it won't happen again," she prays. Sexual instincts must be curbed, she is clear on that. "It doesn't mean that I don't have the same desires as everyone else, just that I keep them under control. If I didn't have those feelings, it would be very simple, but I do have them and I control them because that's what my religion dictates," she says, emphatically.

Both from the same village, both fearful of God and what people would say, given that they are not engaged, the two decide to meet up in secret in Kutahya. Nobody at home, except their families, knows about their relationship, and it had better stay that way until their commitment is made official. Otherwise, they would be talk of this little, traditional town.

In the Tile Museum, she does not even look at him. For twenty minutes she stares transfixed at the famous collection of coloured ceramics exhibited in the display cabinets. They have gone a month without seeing each other and when they finally manage to contrive a chance meeting, the museum is about to close. Only twenty minutes to spend together.

"I'm excited and nervous. I can't look him in the face."

He cannot take his eyes off Sennur, even for a second.

"He reproaches me for not looking at him, but I feel too agitated. I'm scared they might see us on one of the cameras installed in the museum at the Imaret Cami (the mosque). What's more, I'm not even sure that we should be here alone. The Qur'an says: do not come close to sex because one thing can lead to another. This means that you can't have sexual relations but also that you must avoid everything that comes before, all that may incite you to do it. We shouldn't touch each other or kiss. That's why I don't look at him. It's what the Book says. He gets angry, tries to catch my glance, but I keep my eyes fixed on the work of Haci Hafiz Mehmet Emin Efendi, the master craftsman. When I do look away, it's to view the beautiful blue Iznik tiles. It doesn't bother me. He crossed the line once and touched my hand. I liked it but it goes against my beliefs and made me feel bad so don't want anything like that to happen again. His eyes are still riveted on me. I'd like to look at him but it's out of the question. 'I love you,' he says. It's impossible for me to use those words; I just answer, 'me too.'

The minutes pass by. There are only five minutes left. Shall I look at him? Better not. They're closing; either look at him now or that's it. In that case, nothing. I don't want anyone to see me. Another time."

Sex completely overwhelms Sennur. It scares her. Although she would like to kiss Mehmet, she cannot bear to think about what her first time will be like. It is going to hurt terribly; she already knows that. Some married women have told her so. Yet there is no alternative but to go through it.

"And what if I don't want to do it? What happens?" she asks herself. "Women have to consent to our husbands. That's our duty," she answers. "But if I don't want to? What do I have to do?" Sennur struggles to get things straight. "I'm obliged to do it. I can't say no," she concludes, resignedly. "Would it be better with a condom? Would it hurt less?" She is awash with doubt.

No one has spoken to her of sexual pleasure; terrified, she asks for explanations, clues as to what might happen. In the movies, in the magazines she flicks through, in the books she devours there is not a single mention of this theme, which has always been taboo. How, then, to shed light on this great unknown before she reaches the supposed torture chamber? It seems impossible.

When the big day finally arrives, this bride will ask her groom to wait until they arrive home before having sex for the first time. Sennur does not want it to be in the hotel where they celebrate the wedding in case anything happens. Exactly what may occur is unclear, but in any case, it is better to be prepared. At home she will be more comfortable and, whatever transpires, will have everything under control. At least, that is how she sees it.

"I've already waited a long time to have you. When I get married, I'm not going to wait a minute longer," will be her future husband's response.

"And am I forced to do it even if I don't want to?" Sennur quizzes her friends. "Well, I'll convince him to wait a bit. Talking it over, I'm sure I'll manage to dissuade him," she will say, fearful of that moment. "Talking it over, we'll understand each other."

The fact that she has already managed to convince Mehmet on other delicate matters now fuels the belief that her powers of persuasion are infallible. He changed his mind about her professional future, didn't he? Well, he will do the same now. It took many arguments, but she finally managed to get her way and overcome the key stumbling block in their relationship. Mehmet could not bear to think that his future wife would have to renounce the headscarf in order to teach at school. It would be better for her to stay at home and start a family. Incessantly, however, she repeated the same question: "How can I accept not working after so many years studying at university?"

"Isn't that just what the wives of all our political representatives have done?" the young man argued.

However, Sennur convinced her future husband that professional fulfilment was more important than taking off her headscarf. Even more, given that she is so religious, certain that her behaviour and dress would not attract the attention of other men.

The point is that she follows, practically to the letter, all the rules for devout women established by the Turkish Religious Affairs Directorate (Diyanet). If they wish to be good Muslims, then Turkish women should not use perfume with scents which may incite men; flirting with members of the opposite sex is adultery; extra care is required because they have sexual stimulants. These are some of the guidelines issued by this body, supposedly independent from the government yet supervised by the Republic's president. When with men they do not know, ladies must "speak in a way that will not arouse suspicion in anyone's mind," and "in a serious, dignified manner which does not give rise to misunderstandings," says Turkey's maximum authority on matters of religion.

Sennur's future husband can rest perfectly at ease because she never wears perfume, considered immoral by the most pious in this country. The only thing she uses is deodorant, but fragrance free because she would not wish to be a provocation to anyone. The flow of those delicate aromas could envelop a man and overstep the established limits.

According to Sennur, it is a question of modesty. She possesses this quality and safeguards it with her attitude and dress. She avoids being alone with men in closed spaces and will wait as long as it takes to get into a lift free of prying eyes with pants.

In terms of dress, not even at the beach does she forget the rules of her religion. In Tarabya, a neighbourhood on the European bank of the Bosphorus, heading towards the Dead Sea, Sennur and her friends take a dip safe from men's gazes. It is a private space for women. In a knee-length swimsuit and a kind of sleeveless lycra shirt, she can swim without the least worry that anyone will see her wet hair or beachwear which, irremediably, fits tight to her body.

Nevertheless, as soon as she starts to work, finances permitting, she will buy a *burkini;* it is the latest trend in Istanbul, a must-have fashion item to cover up every bit of her body at the beach and submit to Allah. It is the very same look worn by the affluent pious of Turkish society. Stylish swimsuits made up of a hood, by way of a headscarf, along with a lycra bodysuit that covers from the neck to ankles, which leaves nothing but the hands and feet in view. On top—to make the whole look more attractive and also avoid revealing the body squeezed inside this tight material—goes a short dress, usually patterned. With this outfit, Sennur would no longer need to search out beaches free of men. If it were up to her, she would head for the luxurious tourist resorts on the Turkish Mediterranean coast, where every possible facility is provided for religious women. Five stars accommodations guarantee pools for males and pools for females, private men's beaches and private women's beaches. Double rooms though, of course. Singles are not invited. Total luxury for a class allied to the party in government who, in this way, see their religious requirements met.

Mehmet has nothing to fear because Sennur's attitude has always been—and always will be—thoroughly proper. It only remains for him to agree that they postpone their first sexual experience after marriage because his bride is not yet ready. She is unable to quell the fears that swarm in whenever her thoughts turn to that moment.

"What will it be like? What do I have to do? Is it going to hurt? Why do men want to do it but we don't?" she keeps on asking, terrified.

20

Hidden Photos

Sennur keeps photos of her friends and family inside her wallet. She opens them out on the table, revealing a double portrait of each: one with a headscarf, another without. The reason for these contrasting images is that, by law, women cannot appear on university documents with their heads covered. Sennur appears unveiled on her college identity card. Unfortunately for her, whenever she has to show her card to a man, he sees her natural, flowing locks. That is how her boyfriend, who was nosing around one day in her bulky wallet, discovered her.

"He shouldn't have done it. Now he's always asking me to give him the photo where I appear with my hair down, but I'm not going to, no way."

Obviously, Mehmet appreciates that his girlfriend follows the precepts of her religion, but he longs for a hint; a clue of the treasures awaiting him once they are married.

And it is true that, while she says the opposite, Sennur seems glad that he found the photo; even more so, to receive the flattering comments that accompany such a discovery. Like all women, she is happy to know that her boyfriend appreciates her beauty. Mehmet has yet to see his partner without *pardesü* and *türban*, but she mischievously claims that it is possible "to make out something" of her figure and that "my face is always uncovered." She loves feeling pretty, no doubt about that.

21

Hayrünnisa's Revenge

"I don't understand why they can't accept a woman in a headscarf as the first lady of this country. The majority use one, don't we?" she asks.

It is April 2007 and Sennur, sitting on the sofa in her flat, cannot believe the mass demonstrations being broadcast on television. Over a million people have taken to the streets, firm in their resolve to safeguard the Turkish Republic. They feel that its very foundations will be shaken if Abdullah Gül, a member of the AKP, is elected president. If this politician, a devout Muslim, gets hold of the keys to the Çankaya Palace, it will be the first time in the country's history that the government, parliament, and presidency are in the hands of moderate Islamists, something that the secular nationalists are not willing to allow.[1]

[1] The Turkish Presidency is highly charged with symbolism as Atatürk himself was the first person to occupy the position, which presupposes a strict separation between religion and the public sphere. For years, this office was reserved for Turkey's secular elite, who view the reforms implemented by their idolised Kemal Atatürk as sacrosanct. Furthermore, among other functions, the President becomes the Commander in Chief of the armed forces, the principal bastion of secularism in this Euro-Asian giant.

The movement is known as the Women's Revolution, because it is they who head the tidal wave of protesters through the streets of Ankara and Istanbul. One headscarf and its meaning—that of Gül's wife, Hayrünnisa—provides marchers with yet another motive. They refuse to accept a first lady in a *türban*. That would be the beginning of the end.

At issue, the fact that this pious couple would represent Turkey abroad and play host at receptions for international leaders—an image that no member of the Turkish elite is willing to project towards Europe, considering it to be utterly retrograde. Yet that is not all. Many people think that in control of the presidency, the government could carry through its Islamic agenda and turn the country into another Iran.

Istanbul is a hotbed. The sun beats down on streets packed out with people, cries, placards, and red flags with a crescent moon. "Turkey stays secular!" the women chant. In the atmosphere, the tension is palpable. The army—also opposed to Gül's election—appear on the scene, threatening to intervene if necessary.[1]

However, the protests and threats had little effect. In August, on the arm of the country's new president, there would be a woman wearing a headscarf. Official dinners would no longer be off-limits for the wives of government leaders, and their flowing locks would be hidden from view.

Hayrünnisa, the same woman who was rejected from Ankara University because of her hijab and forced to give up higher education, now got her way back. She broke new ground, standing proud as Turkey's First Lady in an Islamic headscarf, the first woman to enter Çankaya Palace in a *turban*. There lay her particular and sweet revenge. The mother of two hijab-wearing daughters, her photo was flashed across the globe. Another image went along with it: that of the other women with their huge Turkish flags, clamouring against the supposed Islamisation of Turkey and the presence of ladies like

---

[1] A message sent by the Armed Forces made clear their determination to intervene: after all, they are secularism's pillar of defence. It came to be known as an 'e-coup' and culminated in the general elections being brought forward to 22nd July 2007. A master stroke by Erdogan, who emerged from the vote armed with even greater popular support, enabling him to swear in Gül as President.

her in the circles of power. Moderate Islam had beaten Kemalism. The tables were beginning to turn.

There was no change, however, in Sennur's reality. She remained condemned to the daily routine of her not-so-fantastic superhero phone booth. "It doesn't matter who's in power. Whichever side wins, we'll never have a government that lets us go to university in a *türban*. That decision would be too controversial," she laments, desperately.

How mistaken she was in her pessimism.

The day that Sennur had never imagined finally arrived. After years of broken promises and with even greater popular support, the AKP decided to throw down the gauntlet to the Turkish establishment (army, judges, and opposition). After five years of unconditional support, their followers deserved it. They would obtain what they most longed for: freedom of dress for women at university. This parliamentary reform, instigated by the party in government, would bring an end to that particular agony suffered by thousands of Turkish students. For them, a change in the constitution would open up the doors to universities once and for all.

In February 2008, the Turkish parliament gave the green light to two bills that would do away with these girls' hats, wigs, and forced studies abroad.[1] Young women like Sennur saw a glimmer of hope, an incredible opportunity. Some started preparing to return to class; others think of throwing away their wigs or cleaning the dust from their books. And then there are the sceptics who do not believe a word of it. Sennur feels happier than ever, once again following on television the events that will determine her future. She hoped that some change would finally materialise, though her words were tinged with a certain dose of incredulity.

1 The reform, passed with backing from the Nationalist Action Party (MHP), only affected universities. Civil servants, teachers and school students would still have to take off their headscarves when inside the public buildings where they spent most of their time.

It was not clear whether after the holidays—because while the members of parliament debated their fortune, the girls were enjoying a few days off—she would be able to return to university without her ridiculous accessories. And it was not clear because, once again, this reform had caused uproar in the country. Identical scenes as the previous May, when tens of thousands of citizens protested Abdullah Gül's nomination, were played out once again. As if the whole place had gone back in time. Déjà vu.

For Prime Minister Erdogan it was the same bad dream repeating itself, incessantly. The same protesters—the secular nationalists—took to the streets. Once again, women's arms raised placards that read: "No to Sharia law!" "Secular Turkey, now and always!" Close to the parliament in Ankara, a city elevated to the status of national capital by Mustafa Kemal Atatürk and resting place for his ashes, his followers made their opinions felt, brandishing giant-sized photos of the idolised leader.

Meanwhile, inside parliament, the secularist opposition bawled their diatribes against the government. One representative energetically stated, "We will never allow the country to again sink into the Dark Ages," claiming that "brothers shave girls' heads to make them use a *türban*. It is a political symbol."

Observing people's reaction and hearing these accusations, Sennur had the impression that she was living through a political thriller, cooked up with an oversized helping of imagination. She could not understand why these women with long, flowing hair did not realise that the reform was limited and that they would never be obliged to cover themselves. Sennur and her classmates were not puppets controlled by the government, but women with a great devotion to God.

"How can anyone judge something that hasn't yet happened? How can they make assertions based on suppositions, on unfounded fears? How can they say that women will be forced to cover themselves or that Turkey will turn into another Iran?" she asked, unconsciously yet repetitively touching the headscarf which conditions her life.

Erdogan's reform inflamed the already heated political panorama in Turkey. And although parliament backed the initiative, the country's constitutional court dismissed the amendment outright in the end, claiming that it would shatter the secular principles underpinning the Turkish Republic.

So Sennur was left with no alternative but to continue with her hat and the phone booth she loathed. As it turned out, she was right to be sceptical and pessimistic. For the moment, the *türban* would have no place in Turkish universities of the twenty-first century.

"It's not fair. Why do we have to suffer this discrimination? I'm tired of always being at the centre of controversy and feeling condemned to this never-ending routine."

22

The Mirror, Long Hair, and Atatürk

Sennur left university by the same door that had witnessed her dress as a superhero every year, every month, every day. Graduation put an end to her daily routine in Superman's phone booth and finally banished forever the collection of white caps that had become her ally. She left them in a drawer, out of sight, inside the small wardrobe at her student flat. It was as if, in some way, they symbolised the end of one stage in her life and deserved to be kept as a reminder, or rather, as testimony to a better future. Her personal, daily relationship with this collection of hats was over for good.

Yet not one day passed before the booth and the hats were replaced by something else. In Sennur's eyes, it appeared neither better nor worse than what she had lived through, simply more of the same. A staff room now played host to her new morning transformation. As a teacher, she would not be allowed to use that square of fabric that, in Turkey, is so venerated, yet at the same time loathed. It would be a negative anti-secular example for the new generations.

A mirror hanging inside that dilapidated lounge faithfully reflects her new custom. There, with the father of the nation, Atatürk, looking down on her from an imposing photo, Sennur takes off her *türban* every morning and ties her hair in a ponytail. There it will remain, hopelessly uncovered. The centre's devout headmaster lets women teachers into the school with a headscarf, but the law cannot be compromised while they give classes to children. Here there are no halfway points, hats, or wigs. When Sennur is teaching, her dark hair can be seen by the rows of pupils sitting at their desks and by all the teachers, caretakers, and administrative staff.

"At first it was horrible. After going through such a rough time at university, then here it seemed even tougher. But I've got used to it. If I want to give classes I've got no choice. The only thing I can't deal with is leading guided tours with pupils outside the school grounds. There, in the street, with the wind lashing through my hair, I feel awful. At that moment all the men, everyone, can see me. It's terrible. At least in school I'm protected by these four walls."

Sennur searches out the positive side of her situation: she does not have to struggle alone. Her morning ritual is shared with the other women teachers at this school, located in the European half of Istanbul. "The parents accept us. They share our hardship. We have their support because they're against this law and want their children to be educated by teachers like us, to learn religious and moral values. The pupils understand too. They don't feel disconcerted. Their mothers use a *türban* and they know that all of this is the state's fault," she explains, while various students knock on the door and then come through, laughing. Inside the staff room, there are women teachers in front of the mirror putting on a *bone*, a kind of fabric swim hat that goes under the headscarf to ensure that not a single hair is left uncovered. Others are sitting at the computers without anything covering their hair.

"It feels like I'm split in two but at least when I finish my classes I can carry on living according to my beliefs. At other schools, with nonreligious headmasters, I couldn't even wear a headscarf outside work. They think that we confuse the children, we brainwash them." Sennur could not accept this. She would not completely renounce this religious precept of Islam.

Being a university professor is a dream that she does not grant herself the luxury of voicing too loud. She whispers it, without believing that it will ever come true. "Turkey would have to change a lot. At the moment it's impossible," complains this young woman, now caught up in the preparations for her coming wedding to Mehmet, whom she still has not kissed. The bride-to-be points out a number of different wedding dresses she has found online. But strangely enough, all of them are strapless and, logically, sleeveless.

"I could put a little jacket on top and then the *türban* which would cover down to the neckline." She will not let the guests catch a glimpse of what is reserved for the eyes of her future husband.

This *türban* is fundamental for her and she will never give up wearing it, despite restrictions on its use in Turkey. Although surveys estimate that between 60 and 70 percent of the population would agree to lift the ban at universities, Sennur knows there will never be a reform that also extends to teachers. "That would be asking too much."

So there she is. In the teachers' lounge, in front of the mirror, taking off and putting on a headscarf, the seed of discord in Turkey under the watchful eye of Atatürk. Supported by colleagues who share her experience, by like-minded families, and respectful students. She does not want to complain but repeats, once and again, that the situation is unfair.

"But it's better than staying at home, isn't it?"

Part 3

The Surprising

"I grew up in Istanbul, in Ni□anta□ı, among society people. I wanted to be like the Europeans. I couldn't see how I could reconcile my becoming European with a God who required women to wrap themselves in scarves, so I kept religion out of my life. But when I went to Europe, I realised there could be an Allah who was different from the Allah of the bearded provincial reactionaries...I felt guilty about having refused all my life to believe in the same God as the uneducated, as the aunties with their heads wrapped in scarves, as the uncles with prayer beads in their hands. There's a lot of pride involved in my refusal to believe in God."

Snow by Orhan Pamuk, translated into English by Maureen Freely.

23

This Isn't Turkey

"This isn't Turkey." Everyone says the same. And yet it is. Or does something cease to be real when it is only a minority affair? Not so, and even less if that Turkey that supposedly does not exist accounts for a large part of the wealth in that other place, the Turkey that is real, tangible, religious. Welcome to *Not Turkey*.

Night descends on the Bosphorus and the muezzins' haunting calls melt into the din of club music. The party has already started on the sailboats and yachts, where coloured lights illuminate the women dancing away on deck. Singing, shouting, and swinging challenge the calm of this strategic strait with blasts of vitality, revelry, and rowdiness. The cruise will come to an end when drunkenness makes it impossible to continue sailing along this waterway, one of the most expensive in the world.

On land, restaurants rise up from the blackness of the Bosphorus, its serenity jeopardized by their sidelong attack. Typical seafood eateries dot the landscape, overshadowed by the kings of the summer,

Sortie and Reina. These last two are the most in demand. Clubs, chic nightspots, luxurious venues where even international stars head to have fun are everywhere. Kate Moss, Sting, Esther Cañadas, Uma Thurman, and Paris Hilton have all made it to the terrace at Reina. Three storeys looking towards the Bosphorus Bridge and opposite, on the other bank, a mosque, threatening to bring a little order to the chaos that will ensue when the clock strikes midnight.

There are at least six or seven restaurants per club. Chinese, Japanese, Turkish, French—the list of gastronomic experiences is endless. There are refined dishes, *nouvelle cuisine*, and the best views of the city, guaranteed. (Its most expensive delights too.) Stunning women swathed in figure-hugging dresses. Commotion. Conversations at stereophonic volumes. Buzz. Glamour, designer outfits, and a maze of crossed glances. See and be seen is the rule of the house. People pull up slowly at the entrance so that their latest acquisition may be admired: a Porsche Cayenne, a Ferrari Testarossa, a Maserati. The traffic jam always helps, slowing down the ritual of emerging from one's car and enhancing the opportunity to dazzle.

Alcohol flows, at these hours, in the form of imported or Turkish wines and *raki* (the country's anise-flavoured national drink, also known as lion's milk because of its white colour when mixed with water). When the nightclub spotlights come on, and the tables are cleared from the immense platforms making up this terrace, then whisky, vodka, mojitos, and tequila shots will lay claim to the night. Now it is time for them, the women, to dance. Not only the go-go dancers, raised high above the crowd, but all of the women, with their glossy locks, bright red nails, and racy outfits. They team slinky tops with jeans, oversized belts that double as skirts, plunging necklines, impossible heels, and tiny hot pants. They fill the floor with sexy moves, uninhibited kisses, group hugs, and whispered secrets in the ears of men.

There are girls who sport less attention-grabbing looks, but they never fail to keep up with the latest trend. Peep-toe wedges reveal spotless pedicures while—thanks to the gym—perfectly toned legs emerge from beneath seventies-style dresses, still short but not such a squeeze.

Plenty of alcohol and the top summer hits repeated in chorus. Three girls. One, platinum blond in a tight black dress and silver platforms. Plump lips. The brunette, more elegant, in shorts and pointed-toe shoes, revealing endless legs. The third, also dark haired, with a sleek, high ponytail and gold hoop earrings. The noses, all equal. Cast in the same mould: the plastic surgeon's.

Tabletops are decked with bottles of vodka in transparent chillers, along with dishes of freshly cut fruit to ease the alcohol intake and cool down from dancing. Freshly manicured nails and long, flowing hair—extensions abound—as they emerged from the salon four hours earlier. Women with makeup applied by professionals. The dress reduced to its minimum expression. Outfits that seem to laugh in the face of the clothing norms in this Muslim-majority country where over 60 percent of women cover themselves with a headscarf for religious reasons. This is the counter position, the reaction to hijab-wearing Turkey. The antithesis. The other extreme, which sometimes even oversteps European codes of decency. It is femininity raised to full throttle.

For those who can afford it, the club route is taken by boat to avoid those lines of cars, gridlocked for hours as they pass through the Ortaköy neighbourhood. There, the yachts moor at Angelique, an all-white nightspot that seems to dip into the Bosphorus from upon high. Huge exterior mirrors transport the mosque, near the bridge linking Asia with Europe, to this unholy ground. At the other side, you can almost make out the Topkapi Palace and Hagia Sofia. White bars and twenty-six-year-old girls, impeccably dressed. Less dancing.

Beyond the maritime route, this time on foot, are the white lounges of the London-styled Supper Club. Barefoot women wander through the very coolest atmosphere with drinks in their hands. At Black (yet another "in" bar), girls head onstage clad in elegance and sophistication.

Between one drink and another, one dance and the next, a visit to the refreshments service in the bathrooms is in order for a quick chance to reapply mascara, eye shadow, blush, and lipstick. Gossip about the guy who threw her a glance and what he said, and agreement among friends on the best next step. A lot of mirrors, a lot of "who's wearing what," a lot of Christmas sequins. The aroma of perfume, restrooms, beauty products, and lots, absolutely loads, of alcohol.

For some, the night draws to a close snacking on *manti* (Turkish ravioli), *durüm kebab,* or hamburgers, and for others, in bed. One-night stands do exist here, although it is not something widespread. Those who make it to dawn, and have the right contacts, can keep going. It is rumoured that, in some clubs, VIP lounges exist where everything is possible well into the next day.

On Sundays, during the day, the fun continues on the island of Galatasaray at Suada, a club in the middle of the Bosphorus with an air of Ibiza, full of chill-out music and huge white daybeds. There are Balinese loungers in a saltwater pool, where people play backgammon and drink cocktails. Here, the Turkish girls dance in trendy bikinis and the latest trikinis. Whatever happened to the *burkinis* worn by the most pious? Their bodies, worked into shape over the winter, move to the rhythm of the music at a concert organised by J&B. The whisky brand's hostesses, all in miniskirts and backless tops, serve mojitos around the pool. Meanwhile, huge cargo ships cross the Bosphorus, their pace slow and deliberate as ever, are unmoved by so much partying.

24

Well-To-Do Girls from Nişantaşı

The alarm clock goes off on the mobile. It is the melody to one of the trendiest songs in Turkey at the minute. She wakes up and with half-opened eyes feels around for the phone, which must be recharging. Finding it, she opens her eyes and presses the snooze button, then curls back up and carries on dreaming. Five minutes later, the same tune brings her back to reality. The same operation is repeated, this time without even opening both eyes. One is enough. "Five minutes, just five minutes longer," she promises to herself, silently. Yet she will not wake up until the very last chord before being forced to reprogramme the alarm. Half an hour has already passed since this ritual got underway.

She stretches out upon her white sheets. A pounding head and that bitter taste in her mouth reminded her that last night—or rather, this morning as it was already light when she went to bed—had involved too much drinking. She feels around for an aspirin in the drawer of the bedside table, hoping that it might free her of this terrible migraine. Slender fingers with perfectly varnished red nails explore the messy little compartment until they finally strike the medicine. But then it dawns on her that yesterday—well, today—she did not bring a bottle of water into her room before going to bed. There is no alternative but to get up. Barefoot and still half-asleep, she pads down the hall into the kitchen. Pumping hard on the dispenser, she fills a glass with filtered water and gulps down the tablet.

Within no time, she is back in bed but suddenly the phone rings. Absolutely exhausted, it is impossible to pick up. A quick glance at her watch, however, reveals that it is already twenty to two. "Oh, nooo!" The plan was to eat with friends at the new shopping centre in Nişantaşı at half past two. She is not sure that she can make it. Getting dressed cannot be rushed and she calmly deliberates the most appropriate look. After all, this is lunch at It's Just a Joke—at that time, the city's trendiest restaurant.

"What shall I wear?" No idea. "Well, something informal, but not too much." She opts for skinny jeans with a pair of white Converse, a cream-coloured silk shirt, and a green jacket. "I think I'd rather lose the shirt and go for something a bit more fitted in black. You can never go wrong with black, although it might be too much at this time of day. I'd be better off in a white shirt and my brown suede jacket, with the striped shoes I bought the other day." Makeup is kept to a minimum, her olive skin requiring little assistance. She then grabs her faux Louis Vuitton bag, a perfect imitation bought a year ago at the Kapali Carsi (the Grand Bazaar), and rushes out of the door. Already in the street, she remembers that she had not put on any perfume, so runs back home and dabs on a few drops of Armani Mania. Whether fake or the genuine article is unclear; in Turkey it seems difficult to tell.

Outside once more, she heads up the slope leading to the centre of Nişantaşı, shopping quarter par excellence for Istanbul's well-heeled upper class. The little cobbles that form the pavement wobble underfoot. On more than one occasion, her heel has got caught between two of these rectangular stones. She strolls along, taking in the window displays of the fashion stores, leaving behind a little confectioners and tearooms whose pastries would tempt anyone. Continuing, she passes Mudo Concept, one of the Turkish fashion brands, and Zara, the Spanish multinational. Finally, she reaches the new shopping centre. Two doormen, dressed in knee-length red frock coats and top hats, welcome the Porsche Cayennes and Audi Q7s that crowd the entrance, anxious to escape the traffic.

She goes through and runs up the escalators, leaving behind Dolce & Gabbana, Purificación Garcia, and DKNY. The top floor of the shopping centre turns out to be full of restaurants. In one corner, a black wall and huge transparent plastic form promise a unique setting once inside. She heads on. It looks like a market; wooden boxes filled with red and green peppers, along with all kinds of different vegetables crowd the entrance. To the left is the kitchen, visible to the public. The maître comes across to greet her, as do the waiters. She knows them all. In the distance, you can make out the tables—each a different shape and colour—packed with diners. The bar is to the right. It is the most sophisticated of venues; the interior designer travelled the world over in search of original ideas and clearly found them. Nothing matches anything—therein lies the crux of the design—yet the overall result is a surrealist kind of harmony. Different styles, a mix of furniture—both antique and modern, mismatched sizes, and the most diverse materials—fill the space. In one part of the restaurant, a string light hangs from the ceiling, not a lampshade in sight. A low wall covered in floral-print cushions serves as a seat alongside a regency table. Plastic seats and Louis XVI chairs surround tables. It seems impossible, but the mix is pleasing to the eye. As too are most of the people flaunting around the place. Many are Turkish celebrities, others businessmen, and plenty are society wives, who have overdosed on Botox and lip plumping.

Her friends are already seated, waiting for her.

"I'm so sorry. I slept in. Went to bed a bit late," apologises Ayse, still hungover. Her constant smile, with dazzling teeth, is capable of cheering anyone's mood, instantly convincing them to forgive her.

Ayse is twenty-six, like the friends she is sitting with today. All of them work. Her job is in a company's marketing department and, although she spends too many hours at the office, she would not consider for a second giving up her professional career. Ayse enjoys forming part of that statistical minority of workingwomen in Turkey, who make up just 24.9 percent of the female population.[17] She could not stand being like some of women sitting here, dressed to the nines in the latest Prada outfits, who dedicate their lives solely to shopping.

"There are too many women in this country who don't work. They're still of the view that you have to search out a good husband and stay at home. Even those who've been to university," she explains.

It is true that, in Istanbul, many middle or upper-class women use all their charms to find a fine husband who can keep them so they do not have to work. In fact, almost half of all women with an education believe that economic independence is unnecessary and that their place is in the home.[18] But Ayse is very clear; she wants a fulfilling professional career. After all, that is why she went to university, studied for five years, and speaks two languages.

"I couldn't be like that. I'd get so bored! I couldn't bear watching TV all day and then going shopping. But there are plenty of women who feel fulfilled doing that," she confesses, flicking back a strand of shiny, jet-black hair from her cheek.

This young woman claims that she is not out for a good catch, like other girls. Mind you, she does point out that the person with whom she will share the rest of her life, when the moment comes, will have to be from the same social and economic background as her.

Ayse works hard at her office every day to earn a decent salary that can cover all her whims and avoid depending on anyone financially. "I'm free to do whatever I want. I live alone and I'm completely independent. What do I need a man for?"

Ayse is just one among the well-to-do girls of Istanbul from the Nişantaşı neighbourhood. But, unlike many others, she is not obsessed with getting married as soon as possible, and even less so, making a business of marriage.

"No one pressures me; neither my parents nor the people around me. I'll get married the day I find my other half, the day I fall hopelessly in love with a guy. Neither before nor after. I'm in no rush and if it doesn't happen, then I'll stay single. What can I do? If other girls choose to get together with someone for money, that's not my problem. I'm not like that."

25

A Nation of Housewives

Among Turkey's new generation of urban young women, a significant number neither want to work nor gain financial independence. In fact, 50 percent of teenagers consider their place to be at their husband's side, in the home, bringing up their children.[19] Despite their education, many university graduates choose to become housewives. They are genuinely obsessed with marriage, with getting wed at the earliest opportunity and, if possible, with someone of high social standing.

The truth is that the few who decide to work have a difficult time of it. Not only because their salaries are 30 percent lower than those of men,[1] but also because those with greater professional ambition will end up crashing headlong into that glass ceiling that still separates male and female in the race for executive posts. Indeed, only 30 percent of workingwomen are employed in a professional or skilled role.[20]

However, it is surprising to note that although it still occupies position 121 in a gender inequality ranking of 128 countries,[21] the Turkish Republic was a pioneer in terms of women's liberation. The

[1] 30% less according to the World Economic Forum, 2007.

right to vote and be elected as members of parliament was acquired here in 1934, a few years before Italy and France and only three years after Spain. It also seems paradoxical that a woman should have governed this country before Angela Merkel had emerged on the scene or anyone had sounded out Hillary Clinton's name as a possible candidate for the US presidency. Tansu Çiller was the prime minister who brought a feminine touch to this traditionally male-dominated Republic,[1] though many prefer not to recall her government, plagued as it was by scandal and corruption.

Nowadays, and despite that glass ceiling, Turkey's main business association even has a chairwoman, Arzuhan Yalçindag, in a role traditionally reserved for men. The reigns of the judiciary have been in the hands of two other women: Sumru Çortoglu, chief justice of the council of state, and Tülay Tagcu, who was president of the constitutional court.

Of the forty richest people in Turkey, four wear executive heels.[2] However, finding a woman at a board-level post is a very rare occurrence.[3] One exception is Güler Sabanci, who chairs Sabanci Holding, an important family-controlled group with operations in the tourism, textiles, food, finance, and tobacco industries.

Few women decide to start up their own businesses, though associations such as Kadiger do everything possible to increase that number. Despite these efforts, only 12.5 percent of those who work opt to run their own firm, compared with a European average of 30 percent.[22]

Revolutionary as this country may have been in its early acknowledgment of women's rights, evolution seems to have stopped there. Today, their presence in public institutions is practically nonexistent.[4] And although in the last general elections the miserly number

---

1 Tansu Ciller was Turkish Prime Minister from 1993-1996.

2 According to Forbes Magazine, Semahat Arsel, Suna Kirac, Filiz Sahenek and Sema Isil Dogan are among the forty richest people in Turkey.

3 Only 7% of Turkish women hold senior executive posts in companies, according to the World Economic Forum report – *The Global Gender Gap Index* - published in 2007.

4 In city councils the proportion is tiny, at just 2.05%, according to a report provided by the NGO, KAMER, with combined figures from 2006 and 2007.

of female members increased from 4.4 percent to 9.1 percent,[1] this was thanks only to the extraordinary efforts made by feminist groups.

The 2007 elections were considered key for women's expansion into the political arena but reality fell very much short of expectations. Feminist organisations mobilised to a huge extent in the hope of gaining more parliamentary seats. KADER, a group that aims to promote female participation in the centres of power, launched an advertising campaign across a whole range of media. In the ad, prominent women in Turkish society—from actresses to elite athletes or entrepreneurs—appeared with a moustache, and asked, "Do we have to be men to be members of parliament?" Despite attracting both national and international attention, the campaign had a limited impact in the end. These elections, which had seemed so promising, brought scant results. The political parties did not include many women on their lists, and the few who did manage to stand as candidates occupied the last places, considerably reducing their chances of being elected.

As a result, many asked that a quota system be introduced in order to guarantee a minimum number of female representatives. Members who could fight from within to solve the problems facing their fellow women, in a country where one in three is a victim of domestic violence, honour crimes exist, and some girls even lack basic education. But they did not have much success; influential jobs and parliamentary seats continue to be the private reserve of men.

---

1 Turkey is ranked 150 out of 168 countries with female parliamentary representation.

26

The Father of the Turks

Seated around one of the wooden tables in that avant-garde restaurant, Ayse and her friends catch up on their latest buys. They then turn to the inevitable conversation at this time in Istanbul among any who pride themselves on being staunch defenders of secularism.

"I hate them," says our olive-skinned protagonist. "I hate this government. But...what do they think they're doing? Do they really believe they can trick us? It's clear to anyone that they have a hidden Islamic agenda and they'll turn us into another Iran or Saudi Arabia." Obviously, she is talking about the moderate Islamic group governing Turkey, the Justice and Development Party (AKP). Led by the devout Recep Tayyip Erdogan, it has guided the nation's destiny since 2002.

"Atatürk did very good things for this country. He modernised it, and now this government wants us to go backwards, to the Dark Ages. He changed the alphabet, gave more freedom to women, transformed the way we dress, making it more Westernised. He gave this country a more liberal and European air. Now, the AKP want to end all of that, impose Sharia law and cover us up with a headscarf. They have no respect for Atatürk," Ayse spits out, angrily.

Mustafa Kemal Atatürk, father of the Republic, revered as a god by many Turks regardless of their political affiliations, broke with a past linked to the sultanates and did his utmost to abolish all reminder of it. He relegated religion to the private sphere, swapped Arabic script for a new alphabet (very similar to Latin text), and most of all, introduced a series of reforms aimed at women's liberation. Even today, Turkish feminists consider them vital. This much-admired Turkish leader brought women into society after centuries confined in their homes. They were given the right to vote, declared equal before the law, and allowed to stand for parliament. Atatürk wanted them to modernise, to follow European standards.[23] In fact, one of his step-daughters, Sabiha Gökcen, became the first female fighter pilot in the world.

Ayse continues shaping her fears into words. "The headscarf has now become a political symbol of Islam. All the women who support the AKP wear one, and in the end, what they want is to make us use it as well. Or do you really think if they start going to university they're not going to pressure girls like us who don't wear one? People will end up thinking that's the normal way to dress and not this," she points to herself.

"Yes, they force their wives to cover up and even pay them to wear a *türban*, using women to carry out their Islamic political agenda," says Burce, another olive-skinned beauty with a perfect French manicure decorating her nails.

"If they let women go to university in headscarves, it will only be the beginning. The AKP has turned into a radical and dangerous Islamic movement with a perfectly studied plan to change Turkey," warns Ayse.

"They want to put an end to the secular system and impose Sharia law. It's clear," echoes her friend.

In the restaurant where these girls are chatting, there is not a single woman wearing a headscarf. Nor are there many to be seen in the streets of Nişantaşı, normally frequented by the country's secular elite as the focus point for international luxury brands such as Louis Vuitton, Roberto Cavalli, or Tod's. Designer labels only apt for the deepest of pockets, which until now have always been in the trousers of the "White Turks," the traditional upper-class of Istanbul and Ankara, non-religious and raised in line with European values.

The country's oligarchy, in control of the judiciary and the army, now writhe at the sight of a new bourgeoisie who aim to usurp their power.

"They daren't come here. They know that we'd glare at them. What's more, they wouldn't dream of going anywhere that sells alcohol. I don't want anyone looking down on me for drinking either; I'd be annoyed if they viewed me disapprovingly. Where they do go is to the Louis Vuitton shop. It's full of women in turbans with money. Now it's their turn!" says Ayse, a touch spitefully.

In the early eighties, during Turgut Ozal's government, a new bourgeoisie emerged in Turkey. Conservative, with deeply held religious beliefs, they hailed from furthest Anatolia and made their money with flourishing businesses in furniture, textiles, and the food industry. These are the so-called Anatolian Tigers, in whose businesses Islamic principles are followed and people pray five times a day. They have managed to combine Qur'anic beliefs, which prohibit interest-bearing loans, with a breed of capitalism defined by some as "'Islamic Calvinism.'"[24] Here are the voters of the moderate Islamists, the AKP. And it is their wives ––many in designer headscarves–who now dare to walk the streets of Nişantaşı or head to the modern shopping centres, Kanyon or Istinye Park, though not without the disapproving gaze of those women who do not cover their heads. The fact that they now frequent these centres, off-limits to them until recently, has set the secular old guard on alert. They believe that the number of women using a hijab has been growing nonstop since this Islam-inclined conservative party came to power. It is a logical perception, but one that does not correspond to reality.[1]

"Women who wear a *türban* don't bother me; what annoys me is their mentality. They are completely traditional, religious, and

[1] In *Religion, Society and Politics in a Changing Turkey*, a book published in August 2007 by the sociologists Binnaz Topak and Ali Çarkoglu for the Turkish Economic and Social Studies Foundation (TESEV), the authors point out that 64% of the Turkish population consider that the number of women using headscarves in Turkey has increased. However, in the same study, the sociologists claim that the number has actually dropped by 9%. Specifically, the percentage of women using a traditional headscarf slipped from 53.4% in 1999 to 48.8% in 2006. The number using a hijab fell from 15.7% in 1999 to 11.4% in 2006. Finally, those using *Çarşaf* decreased from 3.4% in 1999 to 1.1%.

subject to men. One of my mum's best friends uses one and I've never considered it a problem. I often go to her house and enjoy her company because she has an open mind, but that's not the way most of them think," Ayse explains to her friends, casting a glance at the people coming into or leaving the restaurant. The truth is that apart from this family acquaintance, none of these girls has a single friend who uses the hijab.

"My grandma used to wear a headscarf. But those were different times. It doesn't make sense to use something like that now..." points out another of the girls.

The waiter shares out the dishes among the four women, having first served four glasses of red wine. Alcohol and pork are not off-menu for these Muslim girls. Two *risotti di melanzane*, prawn salad with Thai dressing, and a platter of *affettati* (Italian cured meats) are placed on the table. International delights befitting any trend-setting eatery worth its salt in Istanbul, far removed from traditional Turkish cuisine.

"It looks great! I'm crazy about this *risotto*, I order it every time I come here," enthuses Ayse, with her ever-present smile and cheer.

Speaking of *risotto*, the interior minister in the Justice and Development Party's moderate government, Osmán Günes, was likewise dazzled by this traditional Italian rice dish. Yet he will never eat it again. At an official dinner, he called the chef to enquire about the recipe for this exquisite delicacy. The secret: a glass of white wine during cooking. Outraged, the Minister ended up yelling at his host; as a devout Muslim he does not eat anything containing a drop of alcohol, even though it evaporated during cooking.[25]

"Mine's fantastic too," replies the only blond girl of the group, tasting a little *bresaola*.

"Let's make a toast!"

"*Şerefe*," (meaning in your honour). They raise their glasses.

27

Counterfeits

The women kiss each other good-bye at the shopping centre exit, and Ayse heads towards one of her favourite businesses; a shoemakers where they copy designer stilettos. This time she has a clipping showing a pair of high heels by the Italian brand Gucci, which she saw in a magazine and cannot stop thinking about. In Turkey, everything is susceptible to being faked if leather or jewellery are involved.

In the tiny store, down one of the narrow streets in Nişantaşı, Ayse goes through every last detail of the shoes. They will be ready in two weeks, an exact copy, using the leather so abundant and cheap in this country. But they will cost four times less than the original pair.

"I'm spending my whole salary here," she says to the owner then exits through the shop doorway as cheerful as ever.

Night begins to fall. In the distance, the voices of the muezzins can be heard ringing out from the countless mosques whose sharp points pierce the Istanbul sky. Ayse does not seem to notice the call to prayer in her neighbourhood of Nişantaşı. In fact, she completely ignores it. Religion plays no part in her life. Like most of her friends, she is a believer but not a practising Muslim. Every day ends with a straightforward prayer. In bed, in the darkness of the night, she thanks God for all He has given her. There is no ritual washing, no genuflections, no good or bad angels with whom to converse. Just Ayse alone before God with a simple invocation, a reminder of her school days.

On her way home, she stops off at some clothing stores. Ayse adores shopping and likes to do it alone; she is not a fan of going with friends, preferring instead to surprise people with her outfits. Before the window displays of the designer brands she exercises genuine self-control, only taking the plunge during the incredible Turkish sales. Beymen and Harvey Nichols carry Dolce & Gabbana shoes, Chloé skirts, Max Mara coats, and during the sales everything costs 70 percent less. Meanwhile, she makes do with Zara, Mango, Miss Sixty, or Top Shop. And if the objective is something a little more special, there are the dresses at BGBC Maxazira. Ayse loves to lose herself among the shops in Nişantaşı, but not so in the alleyways of the Grand Bazaar. She hardly ever makes it there. Only sporadically, to buy herself a bag, one of those accomplished Turkish counterfeits.

At the start of each season, the most famous shop in the Kapali Çarşi brings in the latest designs from the great European fashion houses. One after another, the women of Turkey's upper-class file into Kiyici, probably the costliest shop in the bazaar. They climb the narrow stairs leading to a room filled with the most expensive bags in the world, the walls papered with magazine cuttings of Hermes Kelly in every different colour and hundreds of this year's latest models. None of the bags carry brand markings in order to keep up appearances in case the police pay a visit, as the owner likes to explain. Customers just have to choose, something that tends to take quite a while given that every cutting-edge creation by the world's leading designers is here, within reach of their pockets. Once the decision is taken, the leatherworkers bring the *çanta* with all the anagrams and accessories used by the brand. The women then barter with a blue-eyed young man who looks almost Finnish and is never exactly flexible. Some of these works of art can cost up to 200 euros. A bargain, some believe, bearing in mind that the originals can sell for up to 2,000 euros in the city's shopping centres.

Ayse will not go out drinking today; last night was too long to repeat. What is more, summer is approaching and there will be plenty of time to spend endless nights on the banks of the Bosphorus or dancing on the terrace at Reina.

Tonight's outing will be better spent at the cinema. She returns home and rests for a while, chatting with her brother. They share the flat in Istanbul bought by their father. Ayse comes from a prosperous Anatolian family that could afford, without the least difficulty, to educate their children in the capital and send them abroad to learn languages.

She gets changed. Once again, the same decision process. "I'll put this on...no. I'd be better off going in jeans and this grey sweater. Grey's in fashion this winter....No. I think I'll wear the white pants, they'll make more of an impact." By the time she had finished, half of the wardrobe was on the bed and the other half on the exercise bike she never uses. "I'll tidy it all up tomorrow," Ayse lies to herself.

She hails a taxi. At first, on arriving in Istanbul, Ayse had bought a car. But the traffic jams and lack of parking spaces were problems that soon made themselves felt, so she ended up selling it. The egg-yolk yellow cab descends one of Istanbul's typical steep slopes. The city is built on a number of hills along the banks of the Bosphorus, so it is all a matter of winding up and down, hand brakingrr aplenty. At full speed—flooring the accelerator is the only technique taxi drivers use here, as long as the traffic is clear—it heads towards the modern quarter of ancient Constantinople, where the city's financial district is to be found.

There, two large shopping centres have been built: one is Metrocity, the other Kanyon. The first houses stores fit for every budget, while the second is home to international brands and the most expensive boutiques in Istanbul. Its name comes from the building's shape, like the Grand Canyon in Arizona. It features state-of-the-art architecture with an open central street; the wide river, from which the natural formation rises, flows here in one's imagination. There are times, however, when design and functionality are not allied. As the building is partially open, it is freezing cold in winter. The architect forgot that in Istanbul it rains, the wind blows, and it can even snow.

Ayse heads up the escalators, passes the Japanese restaurant where they serve the best value sushi in the city, then the American eatery Nam Nam, and leaves McDonald's off to one side. She goes into the cinema area. It is Saturday and the place is packed. Even in casual wear the women are dressed to kill, their makeup fit for a party only to spend a relaxed evening of movies and hamburgers with bacon. They are not very religious around here.

The hairdressing factor is ever present, along with accessories in excess. Why wear just a pair of hoop earrings if you can dress them up with a couple of sparkly hairpins, a maxi ring, and three long chains? In this respect, Ayse stands out from the crowd, not sharing her compatriots' tendency to excess.

Few home-grown films are shown at this cinema where US productions dominate, all subtitled in Turkish. The intermission, relegated to history in many parts of the world, still exists here. Over and again, they repeat adverts for alcoholic drinks, trendy gyms represented by sculpture-like bodies, idyllic American-style housing developments lost in one of the forests surrounding the city, and a crazy Turk who dreams that his wife gives birth to an alien. More than thirty minutes of advertising precede the screening.

28

Sex and the City

At last, the film starts. The idol of our well-to-do girls from Nişantaşı has arrived to the cinema screens of Istanbul: none other than Carrie Bradshaw from New York. Yes, it is the opening night of the film *Sex and the City*, and Ayse, like the rest of these young—and not so young—Turkish women, bought the tickets some time back. It is a night not to be missed. She adores these deities of glossy, cosmopolitan glamour; those four New York women who wear Manolo Blahnik, get drunk on cosmopolitans, and touch up their faces with Botox. They love the character Samantha, who lives only for sex, and Carrie, who writes about it while using the streets of the Big Apple as her personal catwalk. Then there is the ambitious lawyer, Miranda, and the romantic and traditional Park Avenue princess, Charlotte. But what do Turkish women have to do with these four divas of the concrete jungle? Even more, what do they have in common with Samantha?

"It's absolutely necessary to have sex before getting married.... What do you want? That we go through the same thing that happened to Charlotte?" laughs Ayse, recalling the shock suffered by one of the protagonists in her favourite series, who discovers that the man she has married is impotent. "You have to know who you're hooking up with!" she argues with a huge, dazzling smile.

She was twenty the first time she slept with her boyfriend. At that time, Ayse was at university. Many of her friends had their first sexual encounters sooner and had bombarded her with a whole manner of details. Thinking about her first time didn't scare Ayse; in a certain way she was looking forward to it, with enthusiasm and a touch of curiosity. She had been dating the guy for over six months and felt in love; she cherished him at that moment with sufficient passion and innocence to believe that he would be the love of her life. The only one. The chosen one. Even so, she did not want to plan anything. It would just happen if it was meant to be. And it happened, naturally and with the same nervousness she always knew would accompany her first time. With the same love that, at that time, seemed infinite and inexhaustible. Yet it ended as first teenage loves often do: in a good friendship with lots of affection, nothing more.

After him came others. Which is not to say that Ayse turned into some kind of Samantha; her sex life bears no relation whatsoever to that of such a tireless lover. In fact, she chooses very carefully with whom to become intimate. "Maybe you've been with someone for years and you don't want to sleep with him, or suddenly you meet someone who drives you crazy—love at first sight—and you sleep with him the first day," she says. "I've got all kinds of friends. Girls who think twice and...well, in general, almost all of them take care of their reputation and don't let themselves get carried away too easily."

For Nişantaşı girls, sex is not taboo. At the end of the day, this nucleus of high society is rather small and everyone knows each other. So, many girls limit their sexual desires to maintain a good reputation and avoiding gossipmongers. There is no doubt, however, that the vast majority know how their husbands shape up in bed before getting married and so, unlike Charlotte, they will not be in for a surprise. The most uninhibited even sleep with strangers—one-night stands—finishing off a night at Reina, Sortie, or Lucca in someone's bed. Many women in this social circle are sexually liberated and seek pleasure for themselves beyond the typical long-term relationships. This is how one twenty-four-year-old girl explains it in the Turkish edition of *Cosmopolitan* magazine: "It dawned on me that I didn't have his number saved in my mobile. In fact, I didn't even know what kind of a guy he was. The only thing we talked about was if we had protection. That was the only conversation we had. He followed me and that's where we ended up—in bed. We were completely into each other. It was fantastic. Afterwards, he called me and I got the feeling that he was more interested in me that I was in him. But after a few weeks, one Sunday evening, he phoned. He was a bit drunk and I realised then that he was only interested in fucking me. In a way I fancied inviting him over, but I knew I'd regret it."[26]

In the "Daring Column" of *Pazartesi*, a Turkish feminist magazine, women lay bare all manner of details: "I slip my hand inside my bikini bottoms and start touching myself rhythmically. But my eyes come to rest on his dick, starting to go hard inside his swimsuit. He leaves the oars to one side and begins rubbing himself on top of his swim shorts. My fingers move frantically. Suddenly, I touch myself with my whole hand. Then, he takes off his swimsuit. His cock is really hard. In the silence of the bay, I can hear him breathing even more quickly. I'm so wet. With the other hand, I start to caress my nipples. I can't control my tongue."[27] This magazine has been taken to court in Turkey on various occasions for the so-called violation of public morality.

Sexual liberation is not only important for Nişantaşı girls but has also become an ongoing demand made by Turkish lesbians, a community that is the target of discrimination across the board. In fact, their existence is denied, though the organisation Daughters of Venus serves to refute that claim.

All of these women are unafraid of sex and they experiment with it. Some even use toys bought in sex shops together with their long-term partners; that type of store is not something out of the ordinary in this country. Turks are among the world's greatest consumers of the porn industry. One study on the use of pornography reveals that this nation ranks fourth in the world for Internet searches using the word "sex." What is more, the national newspaper *Milliyet* claims that when it comes to the word "porn," Turkey heads the list. There are racy magazines such as *Macho* or *Maxim*, old movies with explicit titles such as *Bes Tavuk, Bir Horoz* (Five Hens, One Cock), hundreds of TV adverts for erotic phone lines, hot photos of the artists, and text messages to download porn videos.[28]

However, the sexual freedom of Nişantaşı women, which does not tend towards promiscuity, is confined within the four walls of that urban, modern, Europeanised society. A social setting that even allows girls to live with their boyfriends before getting married and where sex does not seem in any way taboo. It might not be a subject young women talk to their parents about, but it is socially acceptable for them to be sexually active. A minority, then, in a country where virginity tests are still carried out[29] and few dare to have sexual relations before marriage. Where female sexual pleasure plays no part, neither before nor after men's enjoyment. And this is so, above all, because women are not educated to feel that pleasure. In the rest of society sex really is taboo. The scant knowledge women possess is based on false myths that have little to do with reality. In fact, there are ladies who do not know what a clitoris is, some even confuse it with a planet. Most consider sex as a male-physiological need, something that women do not have to enjoy and less so before marriage.

Such is the situation. The television will continue to bombard viewers with erotic hotlines, Internet will provide a direct line to pornography, and the women of Nişantaşı will go on with their sexual revolution. Yet only a few metres from their neighbourhood, others will remain unaware that the clitoris does not form part of the solar system.

29

Photoshop for the Pious

Sunday arrives and with it, *kahvalti* (Turkish breakfast) overlooking the Bosphorus in Bebek, a neighbourhood whose name—meaning baby—stems from its unquestionable beauty.

Çay (Turkish tea), cheeses, olives, jams, chocolate spreads, cucumbers, tomatos, and cured beef are featured at this meal. Barely disguised glances to check out the other women's casual wear. Turkish broadsheets—with colour photos of girls in bikinis—spread out on the tables alongside women's magazines. Plenty of sunglasses concealing hangovers and, as always, impeccable hairdos. This is how Ayse quietly spends her leisure time on a Sunday with friends. Commenting on the previous night, chatting about their work, their lives, their families, and if they have met any new guys worth mentioning. Reading the newspapers that Prime Minister Recep Tayyip Erdogan considers an attack against the country's moral values, for instance *Cumhurriyet*, *Hurriyet*, and *Milliyet*. Precisely when the Turkish establishment accused him of introducing the reform on headscarves and having a hidden Islamic agenda, Erdogan replied, "What discrimination have you faced from us? Aren't you the ones who publish photos of naked women in your newspapers every day, going against the moral values of this society? Have we ever stopped you? Have we interfered in any way?"

In May 2007 the Greater Istanbul Municipality (IBB), run by the party in government, the AKP, prohibited various companies from displaying adverts for swimsuits and bikinis that featured women wearing these garments after receiving numerous complaints about the number of traffic accidents these billboards had caused. Driver safety was vital, but politicians also made it clear that "people consider them obscene."[30]

The most conservative newspapers in Turkey do not show any photos of women in underwear. In fact, one of these dailies, the moderate Islamic *Yeni Safak*, was taken to court by an advertising agency in 2007. The issue was that they did not hesitate to photoshop an advert featuring a model in a tight black dress that revealed her thighs. It was too short. So, they retouched the photo on the computer, covering her legs down to the knee. The wonders of modern technology!

Meanwhile, colour photos of scantily dressed famous Turkish women flood the newspapers on the tables in Bebek without anyone turning a hair. In women's magazines, in the Turkish editions of *Elle*, *Marie Claire*, or *Cosmopolitan*, there is space for the typical in bed images that accompany articles on "How to Have Great Sex" or "How to Reach Orgasm." The glossies milk clichéd sexual themes for all they are worth: "10 Signs that Show You He's Terrible in Bed," "Erotic Dreams and the World of Sex," and "The Best Ways to Have Sex." Once again, a contradiction to headscarf-wearing Turkey. Yet this kind of headline would never be seen in the magazines aimed at pious women with *türbans*, such as *Kadin ve Aile*, *Mektup*, or *Bizim Aile*. All of these magazines have a strong religious message, advocating an "Islamic lifestyle," which means being obedient wives, good mothers, and devout Muslims.[31] They are publications focussed on how women should live inside their homes, not in the outside world. Work receives little mention, and sex, of course, none at all.

30

Flower-Shaped Style

The weekend is over. Now, the tough week of a workingwoman begins. The alarm clock goes off. Today, all excuses are futile; it is time to weigh anchor, no slacking allowed. Ayse has an important meeting, so the only option is to pay a call at the hairdressers ahead of appearing before her clients. After having a shower, she rushes down to the *kuaför* just below her apartment. A regular client, she does not need to give too many details about her preferences. This morning's choice is a natural look, which she considers best fits her needs for the day. Still heavy eyed, she chats with her longtime stylist, the only one she trusts and whom she always turns to. Her hair and image are fundamental; they have to be in the very best hands.

"Going to the hairdresser's is a sign of respect towards the people I'm meeting with. It's my duty to dress well and also—why lie?—I like to look pretty. It gives me more self-confidence," explains Ayse. However, this foray into the beauty salon is nothing unusual. Ayse has her shiny locks styled here at least twice a week, and all because, in Turkey, hair is a symbol of femininity and a key feature in determining a woman's appeal. For this reason, all women take great pains to pamper their hair, sometimes to excess. Row upon row of hair-care products cram supermarket shelves. Not a single Turkish woman would scrimp on caring for her unsurpassable weapon of seduction.

"I'm lucky because my hair's straight and if I dry it at home it doesn't look too bad. That's why I only go twice a week. But honestly, if it didn't look right, I'd go more often. There are women who spend most of their time at the *kuaför*."

This stylish habit runs in the family. Ayse's initiation into beauty salon culture was at the age of fourteen, her mother alongside. Back then, Saturday was the chosen time to smarten up her hair before heading out with friends to some party or other in her home city. At eighteen she began having a fortnightly manicure and pedicure; since then, not a single month has passed without enjoying a professional polish.

Istanbul is teeming with hair salons. There is one on every corner, anxious to meet the female population's frequent and pressing beauty needs. Men are the engineers in this world of women, the hairdressing trade exclusively in their hands. No one would trust a female stylist. It is men who comb, blow-dry, and apply platinum-blond colour rinses to ebony locks whose dark roots always end up showing through. They work in pairs, as it is apparently impossible for the person who is brushing to hold a dryer at the same time. It seems incongruous that in a male dominated and jealous society like Turkey that such a feminine environment is replete with men, even more so given that most are heterosexual.

Plenty of hairspray, lots of mousse. Impossible updos and hanging curls galore. Few clients plump for simplicity, for a natural look, and hairdressers irremediably flee from this option. Woe betide the woman who requests something simple! The artist would take it as an insult, seeing his creativity nipped in the bud along with the chance of winning over a new client, a loyal admirer of his work. Extensions are the latest trend to enhance women's sensuality yet further. Whether real or artificial, hair is always long and shiny, a tribute to the most exultant femininity. Could this be another reaction against headscarf-wearing Turkey? Is that why women who do not cover their hair go out of their way to pamper it?

The average, we could say, is three visits a week to a curl and dry professional. Whatever day it is, beauty salons are almost always full and permanently open (Sunday included). The cost is some twenty-five or thirty Turkish lira (between twelve and fifteen euros) per session, plus tips. And tipping is not a question to be taken lightly because, with so many assistants and second assistants—labour is abundant in this country—along with the gaggle of staff surrounding every client, the visit can set you back a fair sum if you leave one euro fifty per person. In all, maintaining one's luscious locks turns out at around two hundred euros a month. What is more, this fashion for hairstyling goes beyond the older generations; not even university students would miss their appointments with these masters of brush and comb.

Nor is this trend limited to the neighbourhoods frequented by well-to-do girls from Nişantaşı. Recently, in Istanbul and also in Ankara, hairdressing salons have opened for more religious women who cover their hair with a *türban*. The opposite sex has no place there, and although these women will not go on to show off their hairdos in the street, they can boast the latest creations in headscarf tying. Up to ninety different styles are available at these salons. The most popular: those named after flowers. Among them, the rose or tulip-shaped styles have, without doubt, the greatest following, although the price is not apt for all budgets: seventy-five lira, some forty euros. Techniques for creating a bridal hijab cost no less than two hundred fifty lira, around one hundred thirty euros. Who said that pious women were not interested in looking attractive?

When it comes to manicures and pedicures, it is women who are in charge and at all kinds of salons. However, you do not see many hijab-wearing ladies sporting bright red nails, the most popular colour among clients from the mixed-sex beauty centres.

Women also pull the strings in hair removal, literally, because thread is the material used for tidying eyebrows or upper lips. It is woven between beauticians' fingers, forming a kind of scalene triangle, the excess thread held between their teeth. Then they pull on this string such that the triangle, already positioned over the eyebrows, opens and closes. The thread acts like a pair of scissors, though in this case it pulls hairs out from the roots without any need for wax. According to women here, between the heat and the ripping action, waxing causes more wrinkles. Threading is an Indian technique but has always been used in Istanbul too.

Not a hair out of place, manicure and pedicure at the ready, eyebrows perfectly shaped. Only the finishing touch is missing: an abundance of concealer and plenty of makeup. Many women choose to have it done by professionals. Others take their makeup bag along with them and, when their nails are dry, apply it themselves with a level of skill gained only through daily practice. Ayse, however, is much more natural in her beauty routine.

The fact is that some Turkish women are never be seen without makeup or accessories, even when doing sport. As it runs through Bebek, the European bank of the Bosphorus is full of girls doing a kind of snail's-pace jogging, their faces perfectly made up. At the gyms, some wear enormous hoop earrings, which dangle from their earlobes while they jump along to samba rhythms, doing everything possible to avoid working up a sweat.

In this race to be the most beautiful, plastic surgery is not ruled out either. The most popular and widespread—unavoidably visible among young people—is a nose job. The streets play unfortunate witness to these operations, with bulky, attention-grabbing bandages covering what were previously aquiline noses, so typical in women of these latitudes.

Beauty centres with cutting-edge technology imported from Europe or gyms fitted out with the very latest equipment are other regular stop offs on the itinerary of many nonworking women.

31

Men

The setting for today is one of the oldest cafes in Bebek, on the banks of the Bosphorus, where famous writers put the finishing touches on their novels while regular clients play their unmissable game of backgammon. The actors: the ever-cheerful Ayse and some friends. The conversation: men, what else?

"They're hyper traditional. Don't think that just because they're so modern looking it's not the case," says Özgül, tea in hand. She is a well-known Turkish designer, publicist, and writer. Yet she and her fame have found no place in a lasting relationship. "Men in this country don't know how to accept it when a woman's successful."

"They treat us like inferior beings. It doesn't matter if we've studied at university or not. They want women at home, between the pots and pans, kitchen sink and babies' bottles. The worst thing is that it's their mothers' fault. They're the ones who have brought men up to be like this. They call their sons 'my pasha,' telling guys they're the best and that their wives have to treat them like lords. It turns them into selfish characters who look down on us." It is Betul, an incredibly beautiful Turkish-German girl, who is now speaking.

"What you're both saying isn't true. They're not all like that. In fact, all the guys I know do housework and they're not sexist in the least. What's more, some of my female friends who are married don't do a single thing in the house and it's the blokes who tidy everything up and even cook, if they have to. I think your claims are over the top. I don't share that viewpoint. None of my male friends have ever scorned me or treated me worse for being a woman. My boyfriends have never done that either," says Ayse. Such radically opposing perceptions may perhaps stem from the age difference between these girls. Ayse is still a long way off thirty, while the other two passed that milestone some time ago.

"Almost all of them are. At the beginning they're charming but as soon as they have you, the sexist vein shows through. They leave you at home and that's it, they're off looking for someone else." This assertion emerges from the plump lips of Betul, the stunning, long-haired blond, who is already married.

In Turkey, it seems to be commonly accepted that a man should take lovers. Perhaps it has something to do with a polygamous past that, despite the reforms imposed by Atatürk condemning the practice, is still engraved in the national subconscious. There were many years of *Mecelle*[1] in the Ottoman Empire, whereby men could enjoy the privilege of having at least four wives among their possessions or even, in the case of the sultans, harems with hundreds of women.

"We women have to be really smart if we want to hold on to our husbands. After a couple of years, when passion fades, it's very difficult," says the imposing Betul.

These Nişantaşı girls feel constantly forced to compete in the beauty stakes with other women, who some consider to be genuine enemies. The result means long hours at the hair salon, shopping, and a constant pressure to be as good-looking as possible. In a way, these women fear losing their men. In fact, attacks of jealousy are the order of the day. Regardless of gender, everyone seems to suffer the same vice as Othello and, without exception, consider it healthy, although on many occasions it turns into something much darker.

More than once, Ayse has been unable to control herself in public when her boyfriend was talking to or looking at other girls. Clearly uncomfortable, she did not hesitate in causing a scene. "I'm very jealous. What's more, I like my boyfriends to be so as well. All

1 The Civil Code of the Ottoman Empire, based on *Sharia*, Islamic Law.

women find that flattering. We want our guys to feel jealous because it's a way of showing us how deeply they love us and how much they desire us. No one likes an overdose though," explains Ayse, who is not in love right now but used to be.

Out on the town, glances are exchanged and everyone guards closely their most prized possessions. Jealousy is, without a doubt, Turkey's illness, a demon that torments relationships, although many see it as a sign of passionate love. That said, couples do tend to play out their scenes in the privacy of their own homes, if married, or in places somewhat removed from the crowd for those who are simply going out together.

"In the end, you just finish up getting stressed a lot of the time. There are so many things you have to do before going out to a bar that sometimes I just wind up choosing to stay at home," says Betul. "Obviously, I'm not going to go out to one of those places if I'm not perfectly dressed. What for? To end up having a terrible time because everyone's looking you up and down." While uttering this phrase, she realises that our dear Ayse has already scrutinized every single woman in the bar.

32

Not Ramadan in Not Turkey

While the three friends continue their lively conversation on the banks of the Bosphorus, the muezzin's voices can be heard. It is time for evening prayer. The women carry on, putting the world around them to rights. None of them gets up to go to the mosque, which is only ten metres from Cafe Bebek. They do not even seem to have noticed the call to prayer. However, they are all Muslims.

The most that Ayse, Betul, and Özgül manage to do is finish off the day with a prayer, just before going to bed. And when Ramadan arrives, none of them observes it strictly enough to be considered a good Muslim. During this time, the city of Istanbul closes some of its bars and restaurants, and stops serving alcohol. The premises in Bebek, on the other hand, stay open and few people seem to deprive themselves of food or drink. The nightclubs here do not close their doors either, though the crowds are much reduced.

Once again we are in *Not Turkey*; a place where Ramadan is not felt with the same intensity. Its inhabitants do not follow to the letter the Qur'an's guidelines for these days, but they will take a little more care than usual with what they consume. Each afternoon during Ramadan, everyone—rich and poor, secular and religious, working-women and housewives—will suffer the countless traffic jams that build up in Istanbul as people attempt to get home as quickly as possible after a whole day without food or drink. When the last rays of light have faded, those who are fasting will then enjoy the *Iftar.* It is a veritable banquet, where they will fill their empty stomachs on soft, freshly baked pitta bread, soup, vegetables, and the delicious and plentiful Turkish olives. This is the traditional menu, which can be extended in line with the buying power of the family concerned.

Our friends Ayse, Betul, and Özgül will eat to their heart's content in full daylight, but will not decline the opportunity to participate in the succulent feasts prepared in all the city's restaurants and hotels during Ramadan. Lavish dining in excess, the prize awaiting those who follow the Qur'an's commandments.

During this time, Istanbul is engulfed in a festive atmosphere as soon as the sun goes down; the daytime is silent and languid. This is particularly true if Ramadan falls in summer when there are many more hours of sunlight and the nights play hard to get.

At sunset, there is a renewed liveliness after a listless day; a day when Turkey functions more slowly, nothing works at the right speed, and businesses are only half as productive. The city runs at half throttle, the minds of the most devout as well. Some women are exempt from observing the *oruç* (fast). Many, because they are expecting, others because they are breast-feeding their children, and all—temporarily—if they have their period.

These Nişantaşı girls fall far short of strict compliance with other precepts such as not smoking or chewing gum, rules which the population's most religious follow unwaveringly.

The sound of drums reverberates across the city. A kind of trumpet-free fanfare, or even a *mani* (popular, four-line songs), heralds the moment to drag oneself out of bed and prepare the *sahur*, or breakfast. It is the first meal before facing hour upon hour without a drop to drink or a bite to eat. This peculiar method of waking up the population is a tradition that predates alarm clocks and modern technology.

Ayse, Betul, and Özgül have no way to avoid hearing the incessant boom-boom-boom but none of them gets up. Yet these three young women are Muslims, although they do not live according to the Five Pillars of Islam and have not read the sacred writings.

"I know what I need to know," says Ayse, who learnt everything about her faith from her parents when she was a child. They are not strict either in following the commandments of their creed.

It is likely that none of these girls will ever travel to Mecca, and almost certainly, most of them will continue without fasting during Ramadan or praying five times a day. Pork will also carry on being a part of their diet, as long as we are talking about the delicious *prosciutto di Parma*, one of the only cured hams available in Istanbul, where baguettes are filled with cold cuts of beef. However, all three know that "there is no god but Allah, and Mohammed is his prophet"; that they must share and be charitable to the poor.

A few prayers and these rules for being a good Muslim are all they remember from religious education classes at school. These are women who view religion from a distance, but they are believers like everyone else.

33

Brooding over the Same Old Headscarf

Once again they have arrived back at their starting point: the Islamic headscarf. The theme that most concerns them these days.

"The Qur'an doesn't say that women have to be covered," says Asye.

"Yeah, they interpret it however they like. Wearing a headscarf doesn't mean that a person follows their religion any better." This time, it is Betul who speaks.

"What good Muslims they are! They put on a little scarf, then gossip and badmouth people." Özgül also hates to think that anyone could force her to wear one.

"They interpret the Qur'an as the mood takes them. The only thing they want is that women are subject to men," Betul concludes.

"That's right. They are obliged to cover up. If I went right now and told my father that I wanted to wear a veil, he wouldn't say anything. Do you really think that the fathers of these girls who hide themselves away would act in the same manner? I can tell you now that they wouldn't allow their daughters to stop wearing a headscarf, even if the girls wanted to," says Ayse.

"They brainwash girls with religion. It's true that there are some women now who are educated, who've been to university, but they'll end up being made to stay at home, as has happened with all of them," Özgül continues.

Betul picks up the baton, pointing out that this is what occurred to most wives of those belonging to the political party in government: they were forced to cover themselves before they had even become adults.

It is true that Turkey's first lady, Hayrünnisa Gül, was married to the president, Abdullah Gül, when was she was just fifteen. He was already a full-grown man of thirty-one. When she became his wife, she decided to start using a headscarf.

Her friend Ermine, the wife of Prime Minister Erdogan, contemplated suicide when her brother informed her at fifteen that she had to wear a hijab. Only by studying the holy book and coming into contact with other pious women was she finally convinced to cover up.

"I can't stand it that women like that represent us abroad. What image are we going to put across in Europe?" asks Ayse.

"Well, Islamic of course! One of traditional and backwards-looking women," says Betul.

All three state that they respect religious beliefs but consider it more appropriate to leave them to the private sphere. More so, if a religious symbol such as the *türban* ends up being used for political ends.

"They're not better people than us, I'm sure of that," Ayse declares. "The important thing is what each person is like, not the religion they practice."

Religion, in short, does not determine the lifestyle of these girls, whose day is not split up into five periods of time. However, it is at present their overriding fear. They are convinced that little by little, stealthily, the AKP government is bringing moral and religious precepts into this secular republic's political arena.

Ayse headed to the streets alongside the Turkish flags and placards reading, "We don't want *Sharia*," during the demonstrations that took place in Istanbul in April 2007. She did not want Abdullah Gül, a member of the AKP, as president of her secular country, and even less so, a first lady like Hayrünnisa. Ayse shouted and chanted, but

Gül was elected and now presides over the fate of the Turks. She also clamoured against plans to lift the headscarf ban in universities. And she will continue to protest whenever she feels that the government is leading her beloved nation towards "the dark years of Islam," where her lifestyle has no place. Where holidays in Bodrum and Fethiye will no longer culminate in chic parties on the beach with bikinis and mojitos. Where her salon-styled locks will be covered with a headscarf. Where a woman's own home will become her workplace. Where women will not be free to express themselves or chose with whom to share the rest of their lives. Where they are not financially self-sufficient. In short, a country governed by *Sharia*, Islamic law.

These are her fears, and whether or not they become reality only time will tell. Yet unease at the thought of a different future persists in the minds of these Nişantaşı girls, who regard with suspicion both headscarf-wearing women and all that surrounds them. This is how Ayse expresses it in her last prayer. There in bed, every night, alone with her God.

"I wish they never change our lives. *Inshallah*."

Part 4

The Unbelievers

Trees weep for rainfall
While mountains cry out for air
And so weep these, my own eyes
For you my cherished lover
I turn and ask where my path leads to
In far-distant lands I will end my days
White you are, white your clothing,
White your figure's silhouette
White the flowers falling from you
That your beauty does beget
I turn and ask where my path leads to
In far-distant lands I will end my days

"Trees Weep for Rainfall" from the album *Las Puertas* by Los Pasaros Sefardis.

34

The Castilians of Istanbul

The gravestones are as numerous as in any other Istanbul cemetery, yet here they bear Spanish names. A Seville, a Toledo, or a Gerona. In the row opposite rests Luna and, further along, Rosa and Sol. Carmona, Leon, or the ever-common Pérez are the surnames engraved on tombstones at the Kuzguncuk, Hasköy or Arnavutköy cemeteries. Because hidden deep within this Muslim city, heir to ancient Constantinople, remnants of Castilian culture still endure. Not that of the Spaniards who ventured to recover the Holy Lands in the crusades of the eleventh or twelfth centuries, nor of the traders and orientalists who came in search of inspiration, but the culture brought here and still preserved by the Sephardic community. The Jews expelled from Spain by Ferdinand and Isabella over five hundred years ago encountered an open door into another land, the Ottoman Empire, which offered them shelter in their flight.

In twenty-first century Istanbul, one can still hear that melodious tongue evocative of the old Castilian ballads: Judeo Spanish. Songs recounting stories of love are played, their lyrics expressed in this amalgam of Castilian that can still be understood to this day. Tales and legends are retold in the same language, while listeners enjoy delicacies such as Toledo marzipan, *bienmesabe* (sweet almond cake), or the traditional *pan de España*.

Peppered with a thousand and one proverbs and sayings, this language boasts of having survived the test of time, conscious that it would have succumbed had it not been for the unparalleled efforts of Sephardic women. It is they who have managed to keep going, to preserve this ancient culture from the living rooms and kitchens of their homes. They too have had to face the dichotomy of living in a land dominated by people of other religions while unable to have dealings with them. Yet some women broke new ground. This is Rashel and this, her story.

She strolls down Istiklal Caddesi. It is not what it used to be. Back then, in her youth, men wore wide-brimmed hats and women dressed up in fur coats and delightful headpieces. Now she dislikes walking along this avenue, where the only way to move is by jostling among the most diverse of crowds.

When Rashel was a schoolgirl, back in the fifties, the embassies had already moved out. Atatürk and his Republic had transferred the seat of government to Ankara. The consulates, however, had taken over the magnificent buildings in the neighbourhood then known as Pera. With its elegant businesses and cafes, not even for a moment did this area cease to be the nerve centre of the city. It was there that Europeans made their homes during the Ottoman Empire, where they played at diplomacy and socialised in line with Western standards.

Now, these stunning buildings, with their peculiar mix of neoclassical and art nouveau, mourn nostalgically their past splendour. Age-blackened façades cry out for a facelift. The government resolves to provide it, and someone decides to paint them in gaudy colours.

In bygone days, when Rashel was young, everything was vanilla or shades of grey. Yet La Rue de Pera emanated a kind of glamour that seems to have vanished completely. Decadence is not exactly unbecoming though, affording the neighbourhood a wistful air.

Rashel now feels frightened of coming here at night, an area packed with bars and Turkish taverns where the *meze* (a selection of small Turkish dishes), *rakı*, and beer fly from the counters.

During her childhood, she would come out of her French school and then rush off to spend her pocket money on the delicious profiteroles at Icen, the most famous confectioner in the whole city. It is one of the few places still surviving from that era. The sweet taste, together with lemonade, reminds her of those days at the cinema with her father; those afternoons spent with school friends and the elegance that today seems to have evaporated. Yet the red trams, constantly coming and going, serve as a reminder that not everything has changed.

Rashel remembers with longing those youthful years when her beauty shone brighter than ever. But no, she does not miss the candid expression of her face, the jet-black hair that turned the head of many a man, or the gracefulness that enchanted one and all. They served for nothing but to bring her problems. As proof, her life story itself.

"These *Vedres* made my life terribly difficult." *Vedres* are Turks, and the way in which she refers to them is the language of the Sephardic Jews. Because as this city of Istanbul turns its most nationalistic face towards the twenty-first century, uncompromising in the defence of all things Turkish, Rashel express herself in Judeo-Spanish. It is the language spoken by her ancestors in the Jewish quarters of Castile and Andalucia, embellished with vocabulary from French, Italian, and Turkish, and still used to this day.

Like Rashel, there are another twenty-five thousand Sephardic Jews[32] living in this almost completely Muslim Turkey, struggling to maintain a culture whose roots stretch back to Spain; an inheritance they do not wish to see devoured by this century.

35

Trophies for Twist or Rock and Roll

Rashel belonged to a wealthy family. In fact, she came from one of the most prosperous Sephardic dynasties in old Constantinople. Fortune had smiled on her father in the shape of nuts and bolts, which he manufactured in enormous quantities for the construction of practically all the buildings, and even boats, of the new Istanbul.

The standard uniform for Rashel and her sister, Clara, were the exclusive designs from Vakkoo, one of Turkey's most prestigious clothing brands, or the very latest, exquisite outfits from the American department stores. They had everything they could wish for. The family's finances seemed to be inexhaustible, at least that is what Rashel's father used to boast. "What will be left as your inheritance, my girl, is much more than your grandchildren or great-grandchildren will ever be able to spend." How wrong he was!

Indifferent to the pitiless future awaiting her, Rashel was happy. Like any young woman belonging to the upper echelons of Sephardic society, she was educated in French, the language of diplomacy and people of standing. Her childhood and youth transpired unperturbed in the classrooms of Saint-Benoit Providence private school, where

French-Catholic nuns taught girls to be real young ladies. As well as algebra, chemistry, and literature, she learnt how to cook, to express herself appropriately, and never to move her hands while speaking, on pain of receiving a clip around the ear. In short, she learned how to be refined.

During the succulent Friday night dinners, it was this education that prevented Rashel from finishing everything on her plate or eating more than one sweet as she would have liked. She could not risk being mistaken for a pauper! Not even in the bosom of her own family.

However, she enjoyed every instant of the banquets celebrated at her uncle and aunt's house on the eve of Sabbath. Before leaving home, her mother would prepare a glowing and joyous welcome for the holy day by lighting four candles, one for each member of the family. Along with her relatives, who numbered over thirty, Rashel would have the best of times, relishing the highlight of the week. While she listened to the blessings over wine (*Kiddush*) and over bread (*Mohtzi*), Rashel would scarcely be able to contain her excitement at the thought of the delicacies in wait. Obviously, there was no pork or any kind of shellfish on the table, as determined by *Kashrut*, the Jewish dietary laws. Only cloven-hoofed land animals that chew their cud or fish with fins and scales are kosher; in other words, permitted by Judaism. The food used to be delicious at that incredibly long table, where the whole family would meet together and, well into the early hours, sing one tune after another in Ladino.

Afterwards, the Sabbath arrived and Rashel would go to the synagogue with her family. There, the *hazzan* would read the Torah—the divine teachings for the people of Israel—while the men would listen from downstairs, each wrapped in his *tallit* (a kind of shawl which accompanies believers from birth until the day they die). From above, in the *azara* (the area reserved for women), Rashel used to watch as one worshipper removed the velvet mantel covering the Torah scrolls, the leather upon which scribes had etched the word of God. From the pulpit, using a silver pointer at all times to avoid touching the holy book, they would read the divine verses out loud. This ceremony fascinated Rashel, especially during holidays when the rituals included "dancing" with the scrolls containing the laws dictated by God.

Although practically everyone in Muslim Turkey continued working, the Sabbath was a very special day for the entire family. After six days of creation, the Almighty had decided to rest, and now the whole community of Jews in Istanbul did the same to commemorate the greatness of his work.

Rashel was not very strict in practising her religion. In fact, her family did not follow to the letter the rules forbidding the thirty-nine *melachot*, those work activities—in the widest sense of the word—that Orthodox Jews dare not carry out during the day of rest. The most religious cannot light a fire, drive, or use any electricity, and are forbidden to write or use money. Rashel never witnessed anyone in her circle pay attention to this type of precept until, as an adult, she travelled to Israel to visit her sister. There, while her son distracted her niece and once her sister's husband had left, she quickly removed the sheet of paper placed over the kitchen hob so that no one could use it and made scrambled eggs with sausage for her first-born. Her brother-in-law, an Orthodox Jew, would have thrown her out of the house had he found out. But when her niece and sister showed up, the dishes were clean and there was no trace of the crime. Rashel laughs as she remembers it.

Israel was the only place where this vivacious woman did not particularly enjoy those Friday night meals. Just the thought of having to walk all the way home—cars could not be used according to Jewish law—managed to put her off eating.

Yet what Rashel never lost her enthusiasm for—wherever she was, be it in Jerusalem or Istanbul—was dancing. She always danced. She was crazy about it. Trophies for twist or rock and roll accumulated in her bedroom while she learned new steps that took her on to win ever more important and sought-after prizes. In the dance halls around Nişantaşı, her feet did not stop moving even for a second. She used to dress up in her finest clothes and, with her cheerful expression and innate beauty, would leave everyone present completely enthralled. Friends' parties were another venue for dancing, though she never drank anything as her mother had warned that people could spike the drinks to take advantage of a decent girl like her. So, between one dance and the next, without anyone noticing, she would run to the kitchen in her dusky pink dress and gulp down water straight from the jerry can. She would freshen up at full speed, then carry on with her jumps, turns, and hip swings.

All the friends that she danced and had fun with were Jews. With the *Vedres*, the derogatory term by which the Turks were known, Rashel had practically no contact, even less so with women. Only the family patriarch was obliged, because of business, to deal with Muslims.

It was in a dance hall where Hasan first set eyes on her, although she would never have remembered him. There, Rashel was discovered by the man who was to love her so passionately. The one who was to make her life wretched for so many years. He was a *Vedre*, a Muslim Turk. Why on earth would she pay attention to him?

36

The Ottoman Invitation

It was the year 1492 when, across all the Jewish quarters in Spain, town criers announced the new decree issued by the Catholic monarchs. All Jews, without exception, must leave the Kingdom of Castile and Aragon within the next four months unless they converted to Christianity. The reasons provided by the monarchs in this edict were disarmingly blunt: it was necessary to separate converts—new Christians—from Jews to avoid the former being influenced by the latter's crimes of usury and heresy.

According to the Holy Office of the Inquisition, continuous attempts over the preceding years to bring this contact to an end had failed and decisive measures were required. This despite the fact that since 1484, Jews in Spain were forced to live in separate areas of the city, where no Christian was allowed to reside, and wear distinctive clothes or markings to make them easily identifiable. Under pain of excommunication, Christians were forbidden from participating in Jewish banquets or working as servants or wet-nurses for Hebrew families.

Rejection of this community was widespread among Christians at that time, most of all among commoners, who spurned Jews not only for religious reasons but also economic and commercial motives, undoubtedly aggrieved by usurious loans.

The Inquisition's fear that new Christians would be led astray, the generalised feeling of animosity towards Jews, and the notion playing on the Catholic monarchs' minds of religious as well as territorial unity; without doubt, these were the motives behind the 1492 Edict of Expulsion.[33]

For those who preferred exile rather than renounce their faith, the countdown began on March 31 that same year. Four months during which Jews were granted a charter of royal protection. Afterwards, death would await if they failed to leave the territory. In theory, it was sufficient time to sell or transfer all their assets, as they were authorised to take their fortunes with them as long as these were not in the form of silver, gems, minted coins, weapons, or horses. Promissory notes were, therefore, their best option. Many in the lands of Ferdinand and Isabella saw the decree as a fine opportunity to do business.[34] In fact, house prices dropped and some local authorities attempted to forbid purchasing property from Jews. Meanwhile, the cost of transport to get them out of the country rose inordinately.

Over 120,000 Jews left their native land.[35] Some boarded ships that would take them to Morocco; others crossed the border and took refuge in Portugal, though not without paying hugely inflated prices for their stay. Those from the north travelled to England or Flanders, while others set up home in Italy or France.

It was then that the magnificent Ottoman Empire decided to open its doors to the Sephardic refugees[1]. Although predominantly populated by Muslims, Constantinople saw the Jews as a flourishing population that could bring cultural and economic riches to its lands. And so, Sultan Bayezid II did not hesitate for a second in inviting them to become his subjects when expelled from Spain by the Catholic monarchs. These rulers had not known how to capitalise on the added value a community of this stature implied, but he would.

---

[1] In 1492 the Ottoman Empire stretched across the whole Balkan region to Venice, Greece and current-day Turkey. At the height of its splendour, in the 16th and 17th centuries, it covered three continents, controlling vast areas of south-eastern Europe, the Middle East and northern Africa.

He issued a decree which read, "Spanish Jews should not be rejected but warmly welcomed and any that go against this decree, threatening these immigrants with violence or causing them harm, howsoever small it may be, shall be sentenced to death."[36] It is said that the Sultan even pronounced these words, doubtlessly casting aspersions on the decision taken by the crowns of Castile and Aragon, "You call Ferdinand a wise ruler, he who impoverished his own country and enriched ours."[37] He was referring to the Jews.

Bayezid was not mistaken. The Sephardic community arrived to his empire only to increase its strength. They were experts in algebra, chemistry, medicine, and political science, as well as being masters in the art of weapon forging and the use of bronze. But most of all, they possessed the technical knowledge required to set up the first printing press in Istanbul just one year after their expulsion.[1] Furthermore, they injected new life into the textiles industry, not only as business people but also as the best renowned weavers in Constantinople.[38] Meanwhile, from their homes in Istanbul, Sephardic women ensured that their customs would survive through their songs, their cooking, and the manner in which they brought up their children.

[1] Two brothers, David and Samuel Ben Nahmias, founded the first printing press in 1493. Museum of Turkish Jews, Istanbul.

37

El Vedre

In the midsixties very few women worked in Istanbul, and even fewer if they were young ladies of the affluent upper classes. But Rashel felt suffocated at the thought of staying at home to practice her culinary skills or whiling away the hours with endless walks alongside the Bosphorus. She wept. So often that, in the end, her father gave in. How could he refuse such a tender expression, those cinnamon eyes flooded with tears?

Rashel hung up her apron and school satchel to become the bookkeeper at a small family firm, one that belonged to a Jewish friend of her father. Her dedication was unquestionable. Work was a source of personal pride, the likes of which she had never before experienced, and also provided a far from negligible salary.

One afternoon, when the working day had come to a close, she decided to join her boss and colleagues for a drink at a club in the centre of Istanbul. Once again, she danced. She never stopped, unable to do anything else when the music played.

Somebody was watching her. Though not yet able to see them, Rashel could feel someone's eyes upon her, taking in every part of her body. Examining her in an almost clinical fashion. She turned and the sensation then had a face. There he was, comfortably seated in a rickety-looking chair, inhaling the smoke from a cigarette. His eyes, though recognisable, did not cease to observe the young woman's figure. The man, whose incipient grey hairs gave the impression of age, forced a crooked smile that was obscured by the cloud of smoke. He gestured for Rashel to come over. "Is he crazy? If my boss sees me I'll be in real trouble!" she thought. She avoided approaching, but the man stood up. He waved a little piece of paper in his hand, while his roguish eyes remained fast upon the young woman. She decided to carry on dancing, moving towards the guy—or rather, the gentleman—to the rhythm of a cha-cha-cha. Once close by, and always with her back to him, Rashel stretched out her arm and opened her hand. The little white note then changed owner. In the midst of this pretence, she fell out of step with the music for the first time. Nobody noticed.

The scrap of paper was in her pocket, but she did not escape those eyes, which continued to survey her quite blatantly. The wretched note contained a telephone number and the words "If you can call me, you'll make me happy," together with a name: Hasan.

Why would she call him? He was too old, and if not, where had those grey hairs come from?

At that time, it was the fashion among Rashel's friends to make fun of their admirers. One girl would call a chap, arrange a date and then, hidden away at a distance, they would have fun all afternoon laughing at the charmer who had been stood up.

In the end, Rashel decided to call him herself. Even today, she is not clear why. Perhaps it was curiosity, or just the inescapable, ill-fated future that destiny had marked out for her. All three (such a significant date would be impossible without taking along a friend) strolled up and down the same old Istiklal Caddesi. They met at the entrance of the large department store that used to be there, now nothing more than a fashion chain like any other in the modern city of Istanbul.

On seeing him this second time, Rashel once again had the feeling that he appeared too mature, the years weighing heavy on his features. How old could he be? At that time, the sum of her life was only eighteen cold winters in Nişantaşı and eighteen warm summers on the Princes' Islands. That man had too many grey hairs for so much youth.

Hasan, unencumbered by any such prejudice, surrendered himself to his feelings; head over heels since that day, he could do nothing but call and attempt to see her at every opportunity. He was a man with a long list of women behind him, four at that precise moment. Every inch a sultan yet without being one and without living under the same roof as any of his conquests. Rashel, untouched, delicate, and beautiful, did not know how to feel. The only thing she saw was a sign on his forehead in red, flashing letters that read "VEDRE" (a Turk).

So it was that one month later when he proposed marriage. The "No" was more forthright than delicacy might have advised when dealing with a man wounded by love. How he wept! She had never seen a man break down in tears before. How could one remain unmoved? How could a girl fail to do something for that aggrieved soul, her dancing partner for the last month? Because what Rashel enjoyed most was dancing. The something she undertook was to sound out her mother, who did not hesitate to use the ever-discouraging word, "Impossible."

38

On the Margins of Ottoman Society

Constantinople stole Toledo's crown, until then the Paris of Sephardic culture. The vibrant capital of the Ottoman Empire provided an almost idyllic setting in which Jews could live freely and build up their businesses.

The sixteenth century even saw Hebrew ministers of finance or economics, as well as senior civil servants in the vast territories governed by the sultans. Just as Bayezid II had predicted, those expelled from Sepharad came to enrich yet further the splendour of an empire constantly measuring itself against the Christian kingdoms of Europe. They achieved important political posts, worked as doctors or advisors, and most of all, strengthened the textiles and printing industries.

Business was a men's affair, women always being relegated to the kitchen stove and their children's education. There were but a few exceptions: widows who, when their husbands passed away, took the reins of their estates. Among them, the most powerful was Esther Kyra, who achieved enormous influence at the court of Suleiman the Magnificent, where she proffered precious stones and gold jewellery to the wives and concubines of the sultan's harem. During his reign (1520-1566) she doubled her fortune, before the envious gaze of her male coreligionists.[39]

All Sephardic women had to adapt to the customs in this, their new home, covering their faces with a veil, as the country's tradition dictated.[40] Meanwhile, their husbands participated in diplomatic activity or worked as tax collectors in the different provinces. Jews, then, were highly revered, though second-class citizens. Muslims always occupied first place. In fact, there were certain rules and restrictions for Hebrew subjects that, although not always enforced, were there to remind them of their condition. For example, they were strictly forbidden from using green in their clothing or white for their turban, as these colours were the symbols of Islam. Nor were they allowed to build their houses higher than those of Muslim citizens.[1]

Despite real integration in the country's economics and politics, Sephardic immigrants developed their communities on the margins of Ottoman society, settling in exclusively Jewish quarters. "From Aragon," "from Castile," or "from Mallorca" were the names of communities that grew around the synagogues. At their head were the rabbis.

Jews enjoyed the religious freedom necessary to practice their beliefs, create faith-based organisations, and to provide education for their children. The only instruction women received at that time was focussed on turning them into good housewives.[41]

As the days of empire faded and the Turkish Republic of the twentieth century took its place, members of the Sephardic community continued to boast outstanding positions in parliament, industry, universities, medicine, and the police force. Even some chief justices' were Jewish. In a shining example of integration, Jews were also members of the national teams for basketball, swimming, athletics, and table tennis.[42]

---

[1] 90% of the time, these restrictions were not applied by the Muslim population, according to historian Naim Güleryuz, who claims that the authorities were "very tolerant" with Jews as long as they paid their taxes. In fact, they were allowed to open their own schools, congregations and practice their faith in absolute freedom.

However, that barrier always endured. There was a difference, which made the two societies—Muslim and Jewish—develop in parallel, never in unison. Coexistence and interaction, but just enough for business was the unwritten rule.

39

The Wedding that Could Not Be

"He's Jewish, dad, but he doesn't know how to speak Spanish." That is how Rashel introduced Hasan.

With that white lie, she managed to have her admirer admitted to the house, invited to dinners at which her father would converse with the charmer until well into the night. How he failed to notice this deception Rashel is unable to explain even today. At one point, he actually declared, "I'd like you to marry a man like him, my girl." Nor does she recall how her father finally uncovered the fraud. What she has never forgotten, even for a moment, was his anger. The fury that overcame her adored papá when he realised that the man who had shared his table was nothing more than a *Vedre*, an infidel. His rage bore down upon Rashel. He locked her inside her room for four days, the same time that Hasan kept vigil, day and night, beneath his beloved's window. Rashel's admirer was one of those stubborn types when madly in love: willing to do anything to get what they desire. Or, better said, to get the woman they desire.

She spent four days and four nights between those four walls. Perhaps it was the lack of air—the same air she has needed every day of her life to avoid feeling oppressed—that sparked the cursed illness that was to mark the rest of her days. She coughed and coughed. She could not breathe or eat. They said that it was pneumonia, an illness for which there was no cure at that time. Rashel felt her life slipping away, terribly *jasina*, which means sick in Ladino. Finally, the doctor pronounced his diagnosis to a father plagued by remorse yet who could do nothing but remain firm in his principles.

"She will not live long," the prestigious specialist said to the head of the family.

Eighteen years. Rashel was only eighteen years old, with sparkling eyes that seemed to radiate energy and a longing to discover the world.

Hasan went crazy when he heard the news. He needed to be with her; no other alternative would enter his head. He could not conceive of Rashel lying prostrate in bed without being at her side and expressed as much to the winsome patient's father. How could he think about his principles when his little girl could perish at any moment? How could he put religion before the wishes of his dying daughter? What did it matter if he was Jewish, Muslim, or Christian? That was of no importance now; it had become a mere triviality. All Rashel's father desired was to give her the best he could offer, to meet her every whim during what remained of her life, now cut short.

"She will not live. It is too difficult for her to breathe. Her lungs are very swollen." Those were the only words echoing in her father's mind. His musings on the insurmountable divide between Jews and Muslims took second stage. Not that his prejudices vanished; quite simply, there were more important problems to face.

So Hasan ended up coming into the girl's home every day and becoming her personal nurse.

"He looked after me so much. He was madly in love with me," recalls Rashel, smiling, though her eyes are unable to mask the anguish of one who has suffered. Yet she is the cheeriest of characters and has always battled her illness with courage. Hasan used to lift her out of bed, used to feed her. He would chop every little piece of food she was unable to swallow until, one day, a Yugoslav doctor prescribed a medicine to aid digestion. From then on, all that passed

Rashel's lips was smoked salmon and caviar. Refined, even in illness. And there he remained, at her side, every day.

In the end, Rashel's father succumbed. How could he fail to? How could he deprive his daughter when the clock was ticking against her? When death understood neither youth nor beauty? Mr. Carmona gave the word one bright, sunny morning in Istanbul. Outside, the sound of the *vapur*—the boats that criss-crossed the Bosphorus—and the squawking seagulls, flying along after them as if they planned to board ship, filled the air. He knew that she would live but a few years, so why refuse any longer?

"You may wed, my dear girl, if that's what you want," said her father, doing his utmost to contain the tears.

Rashel's mother was there, but she was very American and never let her feelings show. She seemed unaffected by everything, as if neither cold nor heat existed. Always that warm coolness that indicated nothing. Did she agree or not? She was like a statue.

The news reached everyone's ears. Nobody in that large, crowded family could believe what was happening. A Jew and a *Vedre*. And if they could not understand it, then even less so the rest of the Sephardic community, where a union like this was practically unheard of. At that time, a relationship of this kind was considered absolute blasphemy. From as far away as France, Rashel's paternal uncle arrived to ask if she was not fearful of marrying a Turk.

"He's a good man," she replied, unaware that time would prove the opposite.

Comments flooded in from all sides. Criticism and attempts at persuasion. The whole family split between those prepared to compromise and those who would not. Over half chose not to attend the wedding, despite the fact that the love-struck groom did everything possible to please them all. He considered converting to Judaism, but at that time Turkey was not, nor is now, a tolerant country in its dealings with other beliefs.

"A Turk convert to Judaism? We'll be killed!" This was the reaction from Rashel, who was not willing to run the risk.

Travelling to Israel was the only option remaining and that is what they decided to do. Yet this time, the same illness that had served to dispel objections to their wedding now dashed their plans.

There was to be no conversion, no synagogue wedding, no white bridal gown. Nor would there be prayers or a glass of wine broken with the groom's right foot at the end of the ceremony. It was a registry office and her wedding outfit, a suit. And is it that, precisely that, which still hurts now, even at her age: not having entered the synagogue on her father's arm, dressed in white. Nor was there a *chuppah*, the canopy symbolising the couple's home, and she performed not even one of the seven circles around the groom which should be completed in order to deliver and protect him from harmful spirits. They were not given the *ketubah*, the marriage contract explaining the couple's rights and duties; Rashel would receive nothing more than a simple marriage certificate at the end of the ceremony.

On this occasion, the wedding festivities were omitted, and the disillusioned bride set off on her honeymoon the very same day, shattered at the snub from her family and fearful of her wedding night.

In modern-day Istanbul, in the synagogue that is no longer, having now become a museum dedicated to her itinerant people, Rashel observes the huge wall covered in wedding photos. They show women without names but with faces, all in white dresses according to the fashion of the time. All smiling. There is a certain nostalgia in her eyes, an air of what she missed out on. Grooms in top hats, women from the twenties. Men without hats and brides from the fifties, sixties, and seventies, all with white veils and a bouquet in their hands adorned the walls. These photos feature full families, reminders of the most important day in the lives of two people. And she lost out twice over. Display cases exhibiting the *ketubah*, the marriage contracts. She did not have that either. It was not worth getting married. Or maybe it was.

"From one day to the next I became poor and lost half of my family. We hardly had any money and we went to live in a very small house. Obviously, he couldn't give me everything I wanted, but I felt happy, content. Every day, he used to bring me a little present; some flowers, something sweet," Rashel recalls.

She was almost always confined to bed and so he carried on feeding her, putting her to bed, helping her to get up whenever she wished, treating his wife like a princess. "He used to cook for me because, for the first time in my life, I had no domestic staff working at home," Rashel explains, as if now talking about a past that had nothing to do with her.

40

Desire

The doctors had made it abundantly clear to Rashel that having children was out of the question. With the physical exertion of labour and her respiratory problems, her heart would stop beating. Yet this warning could not stop biology and shortly after getting married, she fell pregnant.

This news transformed her mood, until that time listless and subdued. She was happy. While everyone else cried, her constant feeling of being an eternal convalescent simply vanished, replaced by a state of permanent euphoria.

Angry and impotent, Hasan did not even wish to hear about the child. He had no desire to be a father; what he longed for was to continue looking after his weak, youthful wife, as he had always done. No one was capable of masking their rage, they were unable to accept that Rashel would live no longer. It was all long faces and contained tears, which some attempted to conceal although with little success.

Meanwhile, Rashel felt better than ever. She could now eat without difficulty and her life seemed transformed. The pneumonia felt like water under the bridge, a bad dream.

He was in her arms, blond with blue eyes. A faceless voice said to her, "This is your desire. Here he is. His name will be Murad," which in Turkish means just that: desired.

She woke up and, seeing that she no longer had the baby, started crying. During the whole night, Rashel was unable to stem the tears. "Where's my son?" she asked her husband, who could not bear to recall that the little one would take his wife from this world. In his mind, that dream became a nightmare. He held her tight.

The couple both wept away that sleepless night, yet each for quite different reasons.

The only person who never doubted the girl's outcome was Hasan's father. Neither doctors, nor relatives, nor friends; nobody had any hope for her. Yet her father-in-law, always so affectionate with Rashel, told her time and again, "You have a beautiful heart and you're not going to die. I'll find a specialist and you'll see how you get through this."

This time it was a renowned German who carried out thousands of tests and would be responsible for assisting Rashel during the birth. He would not allow her to abandon Istanbul for the next world.

Ten days before the much-feared due date, the mother-to-be went to her parent's home in search of better care, less reproach, and to be surrounded by more of the people she loved.

Her mother still appeared as though sculpted of ice, apparently unaffected. Her father, however, was overcome by tears. The young woman directed her thoughts to him.

"Dad, my husband says that, if I die, he doesn't want anything to do with the child."

Once again, her father broke down.

"Listen to me, please. Dad, you have to take charge of my son, of his education. My husband won't do it," she said, concerned only for her baby, not in the least for her own future.

"I'll do it, my love," sobbed her father.

One February 23, now a long time ago, the dreaded date arrived. Everything was prepared at the German hospital located halfway between Taksim and Cihangir, in those days a neighbourhood for intellectuals and now a meeting point for Turkish artists and foreign journalists.

The doctor injected something into her arm, explaining that it would prevent her heart from stopping. Her sister and parents suffered in the waiting room of that modern hospital while they heard, as if in same room, the cries of the young and delicate Rashel. It was a natural birth and a very long labour. Too long, but she survived.

When she set eyes on her son, the room lit up, and she felt as if they had injected her with an enormous dose of life itself. She wanted to get out of bed, take her child and walk, walk, walk. Or even better; dance, dance, dance. Everything was light. Her baby's chin was like her husband's, and he seemed just as pale as she had dreamed that sleepless, tearful night some months ago.

One of the nuns who worked at the hospital telephoned Hasan to give him the good news. The little one's father had not even been present during the birth, furious at the almost certain death of his wife. "Hasan Bey, you have a little boy." Beep. He had hung up.

The second call had the same outcome. "Hasan Bey, your son is born." The line went dead once again.

"Your husband's crazy," said the nun to that young woman who was absorbed, lost in every tiny detail of the milky-white body cradled in her arms. She explained what had happened. Without much difficulty, Rashel deciphered the meaning of Hasan's attitude, understanding perfectly the reason for such reaction, as well as the method to deal with it.

Another phone call. "Hasan Bey, your wife is alive." The nun could hear the man's faltering breaths at the other end of the line. "And you've had a little boy," she added.

This time, there came a reply. "I'm on my way."

It was two and a half hours before he appeared at the hospital. When he did so, his eyes were two bloodshot circles, red and swollen from so many repressed tears, so much anguish contained.

"You're alive!" Although his lips formed a smile, his body had not yet regained its composure. In Rashel's eyes, Hasan appeared at that moment more fragile, more vulnerable than ever. His gaze remained fixed upon the longed for survivor, though from the corner of his eye, he could just make out the newborn baby. Huddled in his mother's arms, the little one was immune to his father's contempt, his constant lethargy broken only by the occasional, desperate cry. The father approached his son and Rashel, her mind still confused, thought that she glimpsed her baby grasp Hasan's little finger unawares.

"I couldn't care less what happens to him. I only love you." That was the phrase, laden with love and rejection, which Hasan blurted out to the first-time mother. Sweet nothings that hurt like punches.

Hasan promised to take his son to be circumcised on the eighth day after his birth, as Jewish tradition dictates, but he never did so, despite that fact that it is the father's responsibility to prepare the ceremony. Jewish law never weighed too heavily on his conscience.

Brit Milah, or circumcision, was an indispensable practice for Rashel's family since time immemorial, as it was in all other Jewish homes. It was impossible to disregard the covenant Abraham made with God Almighty. The Old Testament, or *Tanakh* for Hebrews, leaves no room for doubt, Genesis XVII stating, "This is my covenant with you: you will be the father of many nations, and kings will come from you. You and your descendants after you, circumcise every male among you; circumcise the flesh of your foreskin and this will be the sign of the covenant between us."

Still confined to her hospital bed, Rashel did not have the strength to take her newborn son to the synagogue and, even less so, set about organising the circumcision rite or *milah*. For a second time, such an important moment in her life passed by without any religious blessing. First had been the wedding, now the circumcision. What would come later? Would she be forced to pay eternally for this irreligious marriage? What is more, in this case her beliefs did not differ greatly from those of her husband. Turkish Muslims also circumcise their sons, although they usually do so when the boy is seven years old, celebrating a huge party where the scalpel's new victim is showered with gifts.

"Will my son be a Muslim or a Jew?" Rashel wondered. And it was no small doubt given that, according to Hebrew tradition, it is mothers who pass race and religion to their children. According to the Torah, Murad—this woman's desired one—would be a Sephardic Jew. However, for Muslims it is the father's religion, not the mother's, which determines the child's faith. In other words, the boy would join the long list of Islam's followers in the secular Turkish Republic. And so it was.

Rashel was not overly concerned by this decision. At that time, nothing at all could mar her joy. She was twenty-one years old with beautiful, long hair, infinite eyelashes, and more than blessed with Murad, her desired. At the hospital, even patients from adjoining rooms would come to visit and admire her beauty. The very same which would soon, and irremediably, become her prison. Hasan had already warned her on their wedding day, "Now you're my wife and you'll do as I say."

41

The Glass that Reflects Men's Faces

It all began with a blind that could never be raised. It continued with a prohibition: from then onwards, she could never leave home alone, not even to visit her own parents. And it ended up pure madness.

He made her change her clothing. Low-cut tops, bare arms, and skirts became a thing of the past. Now, she was forced to hide beneath long-sleeved shirts and ankle-length trousers. A dip at the beach came to be but a dream, a blurred memory of passed youth, and walking along the sands— accompanied by her husband and completely covered from the neck down—her only way to enjoy the summer.

Her parents could barely credit what they were seeing. It was impossible to conceive that this should be their vivacious, modern daughter, whose dress code used to encompass the very latest creations by local and international designers. The same girl who, unconcerned, would splash around in a swimsuit in Buyukada, the largest of the Princes' Islands, where they used to spend the summer along with the rest of Istanbul's Jewish and Armenian minority.

Rashel felt ashamed of her appearance and, on the few occasions she did set foot outside, would pray not to bump into any acquaintances. She could not face anyone seeing her like this.

It was jealousy, simple jealousy. Othello's green-eyed monster, which Turkish society seems to unable to keep in check; in fact, its presence appears to delight. Jealousy is the national ill and a favoured pastime for many couples, often resulting in tragedy.

Hasan wanted Rashel to cover her shiny locks beneath an Islamic headscarf, but his wife refused to go that far. On this issue the girl was not for persuading, although she ended up making do with a mere fifteen minutes per day of fresh air, dedicated to taking her son for a walk in the park. Rashel spent the rest of her time at home under the tight control of her jailor, who would not hesitate to take a taxi from his office and appear by surprise. He would turn up irate, then inspect every last inch of their home—under the bed, inside the wardrobes, in the bath—in search of an invisible lover, nothing more than a figment of his own imagination. One day after another, every week, every month. But Hasan never found him.

During one of her rare, furtive escapes, Rashel decided to indulge herself with a bunch of roses; ten, to be precise, along with one extra which the owner of the florist's added because he found the young woman pleasant. An all-out battle ensued.

"Who sent you those flowers? Who? Who? Answer me?" yelled her husband, beside himself.

Another sleepless night. This time, repeating the same story once and again, although Hasan seemed unable to grasp it. Rashel had bought the flowers because it had been a long time since she had given herself a treat. As dawn broke on that endless night, both were stationed at the florist's door; when the owner arrived, he corroborated the version provided by the supposedly unfaithful wife.

"I'm getting a divorce," Rashel shouted, sick of these constant and repetitive scenes.

Yet she always ended up succumbing. Her jealous husband's repentant tears dissolved her will, convincing her of something she did not desire: to stay put, by his side.

Rashel would ride the bus along the streets of Istanbul with her eyes closed. Hasan forbade his wife from opening them to look out of the window because the glass reflected the faces of the men sitting opposite. And that was a genuine provocation.

The only explanation Rashel could find for such behaviour was that as her partner had been so promiscuous, always having affairs with married women, he was now incapable of trusting his own wife. So, the immediate future meant speaking with her friend's husbands without ever looking at their faces, always paying close attention to what was happening on the living room floor. No makeup and the most demure of outfits. And never leave the house with wet hair; that was just too sexy to be permitted, as it could arouse any man.

Sick of it all, Rashel took the scissors one day and pitilessly mutilated the part of he body that he most admired. Without hesitating, she set about chopping huge chunks of chestnut-coloured hair from her interminable locks. If he liked her hair, then he would have it no longer. It achieved nothing.

In the end, it was her love for her son which gave Rashel the courage required. She snuck out of the house, her suitcases practically empty, and headed for her parents' home. It was not just that Hasan treated her in the most despicable manner—which he did—but that when jealousy clouded his judgement, Rashel's poor son was the one who paid. Hasan vented his anger on their son in order to inflict maximum pain on the woman he believed to be unfaithful.

Twice she abandoned the family home but, through weakness, ended up going back, turning a deaf ear to the advice of her parents, who encouraged their daughter to escape her sick husband. Hasan's final scheme to bring Rashel home was to rent a huge and stunning apartment in one of Istanbul's best neighbourhoods: Etiler. There, his eyes flooded with tears, he implored her to take control of their new abode.

"How could I accept? Was I stupid?" Rashel now struggles to understand her fainthearted attitude back then.

The same day she returned, Hasan forced himself on her. Nine months later, her daughter was born, yet another thing tying her to this insufferable man and his inveterate jealousy.

42

Divorce

How could one think about divorce at a time when Turkish women did not even consider leaving their husbands? The opposite might occur, but no woman would abandon the family home.

For the generation of Sephardic women born in Istanbul between 1920 and 1945, divorce was the worst thing that could possibly happen. Legal separation meant returning to their parents' home, penniless and with little possibility of earning a living. This group lacked further education, which meant that their salaries—if they opted to live alone—would not even cover the basic living costs of a divorcee and her children. Financial considerations, then, obliged them to fake healthy, robust marriages when these were no more than sickly unions ailing from a lack of love.

The worst thing, however, was the ostracism to which a woman was condemned if she returned to being single. Social events were the reserve of couples, so divorce meant saying good-bye to a whole range of house parties, theatre outings, and dinners. If that were not enough, a divorcee would also be considered a possible threat to her friends' cosy matrimonies. A woman of "easy virtue" like that was a real danger, better left at home.

So, most women chose to accept their destiny and stay with their husbands. Educated to keep a good house and bring up their children, they were skilled in the art of leisure and would play cards to pass their recurrently free afternoons. Faithful wives, who had known no man other than the husband they now wished to leave.

Their daughters, born between 1946 and 1970, would revolutionise the customs of their parents, making use of the option to divorce without the least hesitation and becoming truly independent women. University graduates with professional careers could finance their every last whim without having to put up with traditional Jewish men, who viewed the salaries of their female workmates as a boycott of male-family leadership. Times had changed and being divorced was an obstacle no more, and neither was marrying a Muslim.

However, this liberation had a negative effect in the passing on of religious and cultural traditions because mothers no longer had time to teach their daughters. And so, this new generation born after 1970 knows little of Sepharad, the Spain of their ancestors, and its customs. They do not speak Judeo-Spanish, although they delight in Sephardic cuisine. These women now marry Turks, paying scant attention to religious differences, although there is always a certain amount of friction.[43]

Riva, who is going out with a Turkish man, dreads the day when she will have to confess to her father—a Jew who attends synagogue every Saturday without fail—that she is in love with a *Vedre*. If her dad found out that she has had sexual relations before getting married, unlike her mother or grandmother, he would be furious. But these are different times. This is Istanbul in 2009, and the outcome will be no more than a long telling off and few days of tension.

Rashel, the woman who opened up a path for Riva, is now a grandmother. And their city knows less of religious differences, although distances still remain between the Sunni Islam majority and the Alevi minority, Jews, and Christians.

Divorce, then, was not an option. Even less so with two little ones who made her confinement more tolerable and a different home to keep her occupied. What is more, this new jail was larger and belonged to the family, a real achievement given their tight finances. Life continued unchanged, uneventful except for the continuous reprimands about her clothing or attitude, which came to form part of her day-to-day. Until one day the routine vanished, just as quickly as it had first appeared.

"Rashel, a man's looking for you. He left you this note," said her hairdresser one day.

A man looking for her? Another note? If her husband found out, he would kill her. Once again, a man's telephone number scribbled on a scrap of paper. History was repeating itself. In secret, she looked at the paper, not knowing what to do. To call or not to call. She picked up the receiver only to put it down again, unused. In the end, curiosity dialled those eight digits.

"I have to speak to you face-to-face. It's important," said a deep voice at the other end of the line.

"Do you know that I'm married and have two children? You can't come to my home," she explained.

Rashel's neighbour provided cover for the meeting. Well aware of Hasan's jealous behaviour, the woman from across the hall allowed Rashel to use her apartment. The man came into the flat and could not believe his eyes.

"But are you Rashel?" He seemed quite taken aback.

"Of course I am."

They did not exchange another word for over five minutes. The man simply observed her, an expression of utter disbelief on his face. Rashel felt awkward, confronted with this analytical gaze, this liberty taken by a complete stranger. She was about to politely invite him to leave when he began to speak.

"I never imagined that you were so beautiful. How could I? I expected you to be different. Allow me to introduce myself. I'm Özgül's husband. Do you understand?"

Her blank expression revealed, without need for further enquiry, that Rashel had no idea.

"The woman who's with your husband."

Before he could finish the sentence, she already found herself answering, "My husband's not with anyone. What are you talking about?"

"I can prove it to you. They are ruining both our lives. She wants to leave me and marry again." The man's eyes spoke of defeat, exhaustion and suffering.

"But...what are you talking about?"

Although she could not believe what she was hearing, Rashel did accept the offer to pay this woman a visit; in theory, her opponent in the game of love. So there she went, with a man she did not fully believe, holding her little daughter by the arm. The man knocked on the door, even ended up pounding at it, but no one opened. For the better.

On that day, the roles were reversed at home. Hasan passed from the jealous husband to the accused, unable to do anything but admit the charges against him.

"I can't believe it. You, who've always had me shut away in here! You, always so scared that I'd go with another man! And now, you..." yelled Rashel hysterically.

The woman who now commanded Hasan's heart was the wife of Izmir, a rich businessman who, because of work, did not used to spend much time in Turkey. Bored from so much waiting, she used to amuse herself in Istanbul. Her favourite pastime was flirting with the owner of a perfume store in Nişantaşı. That man was Rashel's husband. And although every single employee knew that their boss had finally been seduced, they were all careful to conceal the fact from his wife. For her part, Rashel had attributed his distant attitude over the past few months to the financial difficulties they were going through after the purchase of their new home. How could she imagine anything else if he continued keeping her prisoner?

A whole new torment began for Rashel on that day; instead of imprisonment, its name was loneliness. Her husband's absences became more and more frequent. The nights bore witness to her endless waiting and the days to her white lies, aimed at hiding the truth from her children. Two years passed, during which she would never sleep easy, never again be caught off guard. And over this time, Hasan became less and less her own, in the arms of another woman. That said, he was still her owner and the attacks of jealousy continued to form part of the scarce moments they spent together.

Rashel felt dead inside, able to walk but little else.

Yet one day, she decided recharge her energy and organise a dinner with some friends. She sang to herself while putting the finishing touches to the table. Red was the chosen colour for her outfit—the same tone that had been vetoed since her wedding—and she dyed her hair platinum blond. She felt like a Hollywood star.

"You're a whore. Are you with another man?" shouted Hasan, in a frenzy. It was not really a question, but a statement.

"The one who's with another woman is you!"

Once again, while they dined in company, Rashel's eyes were transfixed on the grain of the wooden flooring, her face was free of makeup, and she did not speak directly to any of her friend's husbands.

Finally, those two fraught years came to an end, the situation reaching a point where it collapsed under its own weight. The other woman wanted to get married, and Rashel's beloved husband felt responsible—or so he said—given that Özgül had left her husband to move to Istanbul. So Rashel was left with no option but to find a new home. And without her children, as none of the men who ran her life would allow it. Her father, still hurt by the marriage he had never been able to accept, had made things quite clear: "You left this house alone and you'll return alone." The selfish influence of Rashel's mother was strikingly evident in this emphatic statement.

No longer a person, Rashel became a lifeless statue, a mummy, a blurred memory of that woman who used to dance to the rhythms of samba or rock and roll. Now she was a guest at her parents' home, a guest permanently staring into space.

The divorce did not return her children, with parental rights being granted to her husband. The police could do nothing, and Rashel did not wish to bring more suffering upon the little ones, so made do with rare visits ending in tear-drenched kisses.

That was until, one day, she decided to kidnap her son, hiding him from his father's violent hands at the home of some friends. This particular exploit could have cost her a prison sentence, but she finally managed to get her own way, despite her husband's threats.

She would have to wait another year before recovering her daughter. Her ex-husband, however, paid not a single lira in support for his children.[1] Her father would not help either. Rashel's mother was always too close, turning him against her.

---

[1] In the old civil code, the man was defined as the head of the family, granting him all decision-making rights concerning the children, home and belongings.

43

Postponing Certain Death?

"I didn't teach them Spanish, I was too scared to do so. On one occasion, my son started shouting in the middle of the street, '*Quiero agua!* Mummy, I want some water!' Everyone turned and stared at us and my mother said it would be better if they didn't speak the language. It could be dangerous," recalls Rashel, in her imperfect Spanish.

Although the early days of the Republic had long-since passed—when Mustafa Kemal Atatürk imposed a single language, Turkish, to unify the recently formed nation—the nationalist sentiment that flourished a posteriori demanded discretion among Jews. Minority communities had to refrain from speaking any other language except that which "the Father of the Nation" had reformed.

So, to avoid adding more problems to those she already faced, Rashel decided that her children would not learn Judeo-Spanish, the language that her forebears had spoken for centuries. Now, her younger daughter complains at having lost such an opportunity, lamenting as she attempts, as an adult and with little effect, to memorise the Spanish verb conjugations.

"It wasn't the best time to use Spanish. I was frightened," apologises her mother, time and again. She now teaches her grandson, trying to make good on what she considers her past mistake.

Ladino had survived for over five hundred years by being passed on orally. Women would teach their children to speak at home, though very few were able to write in this cocktail of a language. In 1992, in view of the linguistic chaos existing among Sephardic communities across the globe, it was decided that all these different styles of writing should be combined once and for all. Now, it is one and the same language, whether used in Turkey or in Argentina. The development of newspapers in Judeo-Spanish has made a significant contribution in this respect.[44] In Istanbul, the Jewish daily, *Shalom*, always dedicates one page to articles written in Ladino and publishes a monthly supplement called *Amanaser*, with every single word in the Sephardic tongue.

In its written form, the letter *k* appears where Spanish would use a *c*; the *ll* does not exist, being replaced by *y*; *h* is often missing; and the quintessential *ñ* never appears, although the sound does exist. At times, it seems like you are hearing Golden Age Spanish being recited; as though time had been frozen and now melts into action once again without having evolved, apart from a light seasoning of vocabulary from other languages.

The simple Sephardic verb structures are peppered with thousands of proverbs. About women, they say:

"A woman's tears are worth a lot, but cost little."

"A woman is the queen of the kitchen."

"Three daughters and a wife, four prickly splinters for the father."

"Women and wine strip men of good sense."

The best are those that voice that witty, Sephardic humour:

"Love is another man's wife."

"Want to kill someone? Give him a young wife and an old cook."[45]

Ladino speakers never tire of using idioms in their language, which they now fear may disappear. Judeo-Spanish is currently spoken only by Sephardic Jews over fifty years old. However, efforts to ensure that this cultural heritage does not perish have meant that studies are now carried out, books launched, and numerous conferences on the matter are held. Spicy anecdotes, proverbs, and sayings are published by the Sephardic Cultural Centre in Istanbul, which has also organised Spanish language courses, with support from the Cervantes Institute, to ensure that this cultural legacy is not lost.

Sephardic music is also helping to keep this convalescent language alive. It will not die thanks to the endeavours of groups such as Pasaros Sefardes, who, through their songs and international tours, struggle to ensure that Ladino survives both in Turkey and abroad.

The optimist points to a future where Judeo-Spanish will survive. The pessimist would say that its certain death is simply being postponed.

44

A Barefaced Bulgarian-German

She got married again. This time pressured by her parents and even her children, who saw in that Bulgarian-German man a new opportunity to take the reins of her life and, once and for all, be happy. Rashel was never convinced. How could she be, if the man who was to become her husband seemed the greatest womaniser to roam Istanbul's Grand Bazaar? Yet, in the end, it happened. "Why not?" she had said to herself.

Another wedding. A civil ceremony again, once more without a white dress and synagogue. There would be no rabbi to read the Torah, no broken glasses, no *Ketubah*, no songs. Once again, at the registry office, her dreams down the drain for a second time. Hopes shattered anew on her very wedding night; when the reception was over, her husband accompanied her home and left her there, alone. He took off, seeking the company of another woman, something he would do more flagrantly and with much greater regularity than one could imagine of any unfaithful husband.

On many a night they would go out dancing with friends, but it was a rare occasion that Rashel returned home with her husband. Within no time of arriving at a party, he would disappear among the guests, not to be seen again. It was their friends who had to take Rashel home once the event was over. He did not even offer any explanations, viewing his actions as completely natural. And when excuses were put forward, they were utterly comic and even Rashel, in her pain, could not help but laugh at the brazenness of her husband. Once, she found him at one of the parties they attended holding hands with a tall, blond German woman. The answer to her reprimands was, "The poor thing had got lost." Even more tragicomic was the day she chanced upon a photo in which he appeared embracing two women, one brunette and the other blond. "But they're men," was the incredible justification this time. "They're wearing wigs." Unbelievable. Did he think she was stupid?

The last straw came when he brought a woman home who needed a place to stay. It was nothing out of the ordinary that foreign couples should visit their home, but never a woman alone. Rashel was left astonished when, having made a bed for the lady in question, her husband climbed right in, first closing the door with, "See you tomorrow." Alone in her double bed, Rashel spent the night in tears. What could she do? Start shouting and cause a scene with that foreign woman in the house?

At restaurants, bars, and in the street, her husband never even looked at her, his eyes always distracted by every neckline or bottom that passed by. It was unbearable. But her mother's advice was to endure it, claiming that this attitude was normal in men and that, deep down, he loved her. "How could that be true, if he disappeared with a different woman every night?" Rashel thought.

It was clear, however, that being unfaithful did not stop him from being jealous. One night, they had gone out with a foreign couple, and while the German woman touched her husband's chest quite uninhibited, Rashel decided to step out and dance with the man. At that moment, her husband forgot the flirty, European blond and, without wasting a second, jumped up to take his wife by the arm, making it abundantly clear that she was his possession.

She could not stand it any longer. A year and a half of her life was enough time to waste on that man, so she put it to him straight. "I want a divorce."

He pleaded, begged, implored, and promised the unthinkable, but she could bear it no more. Her husband was not prepared to let her leave, but a threat to call the police freed her once and for all from that intolerable character.

45

Synagogues under Attack

The advent of the Turkish Republic in 1923 did not, in theory, impact on the privileges or rights of the Sephardic community, full citizens loyal to the Western-leaning government reforms initiated by Atatürk. However, 1942 saw the Jewish population in agony, hard pressed by debts resulting from the weighty tax burden imposed on their assets. In that year, the *Varlik Vergisi* came into effect, a levy pitilessly applied to all non-Muslims in Turkey. It was a merciless blow to the Sephardic community, who paid four times more than followers of Islam.

Some Jews, most of all those on lower incomes, saw the creation of the State of Israel in 1948—with its widely known benefits in terms of education and housing—as an escape valve from the intense economic pressure applied by the government. So, together with those who set out for the promised land with an idealistic spirit, they would abandon Turkey. Some forty thousand Jews left the country that year.[46]

One event in 1955 reduced by another ten thousand people the already tiny Sephardic circle. On this occasion, in the early hours of the 6th and 7th September, masses irate with the Greek population—who they accused of masterminding an attack on the Turkish consulate in Salonica—ended up lashing out at all non-Muslims.[47] Arson, looting, and the destruction of businesses and homes belonging to Greeks, Jews, and Armenians ensued. It was a full-blown riot, with the army finally having to intervene to pacify the vandals.[48] The damage was eminently material, with four thousand shops and a thousand homes destroyed, but the psychological effects of this barbarity on the country's minorities led many to seek out new homes beyond Turkey's frontiers.

These two events underlie the fact that, nowadays, there are only middle or upper class Sephardic Jews living in Turkey; the most economically deprived groups within this community left Ottoman lands long ago in search of a better future in Israel.[49]

Those that stayed are the people responsible for maintaining the eighteen synagogues in Istanbul. As well as a hospital, two homes for the elderly, and a school, they have also created various sports and cultural clubs where young Jews can enjoy themselves while their mothers do charity work in institutions supported by the community.

Turkey's Sephardic community live in relative calm, despite having to struggle against the many prejudices that still persist towards religious and ethnic minorities.

However, an attack on synagogues in 2003 brought an end to that calm with twenty-seven people killed and three hundred injured. It is presumed to have been carried out by Al Quaeda.

Now, security measures have been tightened. For example, to get into the editorial department of *Shalom* newspaper or visit the Sephardic Cultural Centre, first you have to show your passport, then a phone call confirms your visit. You then take a lift halfway up the building. From there, you must pass through a metal gate, which is opened by a security guard. Then there are more stairs, and finally, the door to actually enter the centre.

Fear of new attacks is ever present, even more so in the synagogues, where they trust no one. Anyone could be a terrorist, even a Spanish journalist. Gates, security doors, hundreds of surveillance cameras, guards posted at all entrances, metal detectors, and aggressive agents who seem to be from Mossad are all part of the new security measures. Getting into a Jewish place of worship in Istanbul is now impossible unless you obtain special authorisation from the Rabbinate through recommendation by a member of the community. Once inside, the questions continue and your passport requisitioned throughout your stay.

46

El Mazal de la Fea, la Ermoza lo Dezea

Her father passed away and with him his whole fortune. The money was never found, as he had placed it in the hands of some usurer who had promised better interest rates than the banks. He never owned a home, always worried that the Turks would banish him from the country without allowing time to sell his property, as happened to his ancestors in Spain.

Need led Rashel, once again, to the world of work. She sold carpets to French and Spanish tourists at the Bazaar. A good negotiator, who handled herself quite fluently in different languages, she managed to pocket a substantial income that, in time, would be sufficient to acquire her own property. However, the Iraq War arrived and with it the tourists disappeared from Istanbul. Many businesses closed and with them the chance to obtain the home she dreamed of.

An odyssey lay in wait. New, short-term jobs, just long enough for the owner to adventure at sexual harassment. And, unfortunately, this was the common denominator among all her bosses. Year after year, the same scene was played out, and every time, she would be forced to look for a new source of income. At some point along the way, an idea came to mind that would put an end to this continuous wandering. The years brought Rashel wisdom enough to fake her martial status; a wedding ring on her finger led to eight uninterrupted years as a sales assistant at an optician's.

"I'm delighted to have grown old," says Rashel, stretched out on a hammock, sunbathing. She is now over sixty and does not mind admitting it. "Thank God I'm elderly. Life is much simpler now. Men didn't leave me alone. They all thought that because I was divorced, I would go to bed with them. These Turks are all the same! When my friends ask how I feel about getting older, having been so pretty, I tell them it's the best thing that could happen to me."

It takes no great effort to detect that beauty, which today hides beneath just a few facial wrinkles and still permits Rashel the luxury of wearing a bikini. Auburn hair and ever-olive skin give her something of an aristocratic air. A constant smile lights up her face, as if her arduous past had vanished from her mind. Yet it remains latent in some hidden corner of her soul and reemerges, mixed with her warmly spoken words.

"It was horrible working with Turks. When I was in the Grand Bazaar I used to ask my daughter to come because when they saw her they would leave me alone. So now I'm happy because no one bothers me. It's true that I have the odd admirer, but I don't want anything else to do with men. They've made my life hard enough already."

In fact, she really does have fans. At the Sephardic Museum, the doorman flirts with her while she enquires about the opening times. Turkish men have never been too concerned if she was Jewish or one of their own.

Now, Rashel is at the helm, setting the course of her own life, no longer forced to hide beneath unsightly clothing or fictitious wedding rings. In the mornings, the radio stirs her sleepy body into action, a few dance steps an irresistible start to her day. She kisses the *mezuza*—the symbol of God's protective power that all good Jews have at the door to their home—and leaves the house, swaying to the rhythm of any tune, preferably cha-cha-cha. At the gym, a constant stream of conversation with every last person irremediably acknowledged as if in an attempt to make up for time never lived. She dances Batuka, laughs and strolls along the Bosphorus, delighting in the profiteroles and endless conversations with her childhood friends. Life is now hers to live.

Already a grandmother and with all the years that have passed by, Rashel is not prepared to let her culture disappear, be gobbled up by the new Turkey. She already did it once and her daughter is there as testimony. Now she will not waver until her language is passed on to her descendants. Sephardic songs are whispered into her grandson's ear so that her Muslim daughter-in-law cannot overhear. These are lyrics that her mother used to sing and remind her in some way of a bygone age, a Spanish past, intimately linked to her family's history.

Like Rashel, the rest of the Sephardic community, in Turkey at least, seem to bear no ill will against Spain. And if they did at any time, then history has taken care of erasing it. They jealously safeguard the Judeo-Spanish language, its sayings, songs, and even traditional Toledo-style cooking. In short, their Iberian past. Many of them even hope to gain Spanish nationality. In fact, Rashel will set about the application process as soon as possible in order to acquire a Spanish passport, which would allow her to travel around Europe without difficulties.

Since 1982, Sephardic Jews have been able to obtain nationality after two years living in Spanish territory or via approval from the cabinet in those particular cases where applicants can "demonstrate a link with Spain as members of the Sephardic Community, as reflected in their culture, customs and maintenance of the Spanish language."[50]

In this way, Spain aimed to compensate a historic injustice that, until that time, had not been addressed. This, despite certain attempts at contrition that had materialised in a decree issued in 1924 by Primo de Rivera, giving Spanish nationality to a number of Sephardic Jews. There were also the heroic actions of some Spanish diplomats who managed to save many Jews from the Nazi Holocaust by providing them Spanish documentation. The repeal of the 1492

Edict of Expulsion by the Ministry of Justice in 1968 was a clear symbol of the Spanish state's policy of historical reconciliation.[51] A more recent and greatly significant step was to grant the Prince of Asturias Award for Concord in 1990 to Sephardic communities scattered around the world.[52]

"My life has been very tough," she says, unhurriedly, with an imperishable smile and wearied expression. Sitting in a typical seafood restaurant on the banks of the Bosphorus, Rashel has little pending but to square her account with life. It owes her happiness.

The Sephardic collection of proverbs held a warning: "*El mazal de la fea, la ermoza lo dezea,*" meaning, "The plain girl's fortune, the pretty girl's desire." In other words, being beautiful does not guarantee *mazal,* good luck in life and, most of all, in the choice of a husband. Sometimes quite the opposite.

Now, however, the years play on the side of freedom.

From the Ottoman Harem ... To The New Istanbul

In old Constantinople, the year 1533 of the Gregorian calendar, the Ottoman Turks ruled over a city that had been in Muslim hands since the fall of the Byzantine Empire. A woman governed from the shadows: Sultanah Hürem, better known as Roxelana. Her influence in imperial decisions was unquestionable, although her beloved Suleiman was the visible face leading the great Ottoman Empire.

Her auburn locks, sharp nose, and immaculate, smooth skin quashed the Sultan's will from the instant he first saw her. That fresh-faced beauty and those mysterious, youthful eyes—witnesses to just seventeen springs—banished all doubt from the Sultan's mind; from among all his concubines, she was the one he chose upon returning from battle. It took Roxelana just one night to be catapulted to the category of "favourite'" and, from then onwards, life in the harem would never be the same. The young woman ably seduced the ruler while, at the same time, weaving alliances inside the seraglio and forging Machiavellian plans that would see her become the most powerful woman in the Empire.

With care and perseverance, she fanned the flame of devotion which Suleiman the Magnificent professed towards her, even from a distance, using the subtle and seductive weapons of lyricism. "My Sultan, piece of my heart, sun of my state, star of my bliss, your

Majesty," Roxelana wrote to her beloved while, behind his back, contriving to bring down his closest counsellors, who might cast a shadow over her authority.[53] She began her own personal crusade against the Grand Vizier Ibrahim, for whom her husband felt genuine admiration. The man's own blunders—he mistakenly sent a letter destined for his lover to his wife who was, to make matters worse, the Sultan's sister—joined the suspicions of treachery already hanging over him. These were added to by Roxelana's continuous criticism from the privacy of the imperial bedroom. In his own, less majestic bed, the Grand Vizier was eventually found strangled at the Sultan's orders.

With one of the most prominent and influential figures in the imperial circles of power now defeated, Roxelana could turn her attention to the most pressing threat: the Sultan's heir, Prince Mustafa, next in line to the throne. Reaching this far had cost the ex-concubine too dear to accept that, if her husband died, she would be abandoned within the harem or even expelled. She had no choice but to raise her own son—second in the line of succession—to take the throne of the vast Ottoman Empire, which Suleiman, through his skilled governance, had brought to its maximum splendour. The Sultan's favourite managed to ensure that all correspondence between father and son first passed through her hands. Mustafa's obliging and measured words were twisted by the astute Roxelana, who lent them an insulting and threatening tone. Meanwhile, his father's replies sounded preachy and despotic. So bemired did the father-son relationship become that the Sultan eventually concluded, encouraged by his wife, that his first-born was plotting to seize the throne, and the only solution was to take his life. The young man, warned by everyone of the Emperor's intentions, nevertheless faced his death with courage. "It was he who gave me life and he will take it away." And so it was. He fought unsuccessfully against the soldiers sent by his father and ended up being strangled.

She had got her way. Roxelana showed once more her innate talent for machinations, palace intrigue, and plots. When she finally thought that no rival remained, the most ruthless enemy of them all crossed her path: death. Her eyes were never to witness the faintheartedness of her son Selim and his unfortunate misrule of the Empire, which, at that time, began its slide into decadence.

Roxelana was the first slave to become a sultan's wife, engendering a tradition within the harem whereby the concubines would constantly compete between themselves to raise their status within the imperial household and the sultan's heart. Many women used to arrive from Russia and Georgia. Some were even sold at the age of six or seven by their own families who succumbed to their delusions of grandeur, optimistic that their daughters would become "favourites" and live surrounded by riches, luxury, and servants ever more. They too hoped to witness and benefit from this good fortune.

The infidels' pale skin and long, blond hair was their fabulous presentation letter before the sultan. Once inside the harem, the girls would be guided and educated in the arts of seduction and the spirit. They would learn the Qur'an, music, and dance in order to earn the imperial leader's favour.

These slaves or *cariyes* would start out as chambermaids before going on to become concubines and with time, if their physical attributes were irresistible to the sultan, "favourites." Those who fell pregnant would ascend to the category of *ikbal*. A son made a former slave well worth marrying. The sultan could keep eight consorts, followed by an indefinite number of concubines. He could, then, delight in the carnal favours of different odalisques, though by law was obliged to spend Friday with one of his wives.

Roxelana inaugurated the so-called "Sultanate of Women." In the wake of her unseen government, there came others who took an interest in political intrigue and, once again, subjected the sultans' will to their own desires. For over a hundred years—between the sixteenth and seventeenth centuries—and from within the walls of the Imperial Harem, women held the reins of an empire that, little by little, succumbed to the inevitable dismembering of its vast territory. Sultanah Satiye named senior dignitaries at her own convenience, while her son Mehmed bowed to her every demand.

The beautiful Sultanah Kosëm, widely reputed to be very wise, was finally strangled at the hands of a eunuch under orders from her daughter-in-law. Previously, however, she had bribed palace authorities to make her son the sultan at the tender age of twelve, allowing her to govern as she wished for the next ten years until her firstborn passed away. He was succeeded by his brother, who quickly fell in love with the tall Russian with snow-white skin, Turhan. At first, the two women led the empire hand in hand until the young Turhan Sultan decreed that Kosëm should be put to death.

Even Hatice Ruşah, in the eighteenth century, manipulated Sultan Abdülhamid at her will. "Do with me whatever you wish; kill me or torture me. I surrender. I am your prisoner. Please come to me this night...I beg you to grant me this honour; otherwise you may cause me death. I can bear it no longer..." he pleaded, desperately.

Women, then, who imposed their authority on men, despite living in a society which subjected them to male rule and imprisoned them within an imperial cage of gold. Outside the harem, in the world beyond the palace walls, their fellow women remained locked away in their homes, protected from the outside world by veils that enabled them to walk the streets and visit the markets unrecognised. The *hammam*, the Turkish baths, were the only places outside their homes where women could interact with each other. There, for hours on end and each with their own basket, women would clean their naked bodies shrouded in steam. They drank tea, gossiped, and also singled out the girls who may become their future daughters-in-law. They enjoyed themselves.

The same city, Istanbul, in the year 2007. That exotic image of the capital of the Ottoman Empire, impressed on our Western consciousness by Orientalist writers, was fresh in my mind when I arrived. Sultans, palaces, and harems. Sensual, enigmatic, extraordinary women dressed in exquisite transparent silks, dripping with jewellery. Yet as I investigated the modern-day reality, the descendants of those privileged Ottoman women, little by little, this colourist view faded. It was replaced by a reality much less romantic but fascinating all the same. Less idyllic but more authentic and, most of all, more fitting to the present-day situation in this secular republic with a Muslim majority.

Since Ottoman times, men's dominance over women has remained intact. Unshakeable too is the nature of society, still solidly patriarchal despite the laudable efforts of Mustafá Kemal Atatürk, architect of the new Turkey, who founded the republic at the twilight of the Ottoman Empire in 1923. Although polygamy was abolished and women given the right to vote and hold seats in parliament, as well as being encouraged to study and work, the majority still remain subjected to their fathers, brothers, or husbands. This is illustrated by horrifying data such as the fact that, in Turkey, one in three women suffers domestic violence, stoically bearing this situation as they feel the beatings are deserved. Many are unaware of their rights, most of the time through lack of education. In fact, when abused, they consider it something normal and so do not tell anyone. If they do seek help then it is from their mothers who, as a general rule, recommend their daughters to keep quiet. There is still a huge number of women who do not report this kind of abuse through fear of their husbands, lack of resources, or because the authorities offer no solution to their problems.[54] Turkish women's organisations claim that this phenomenon "is widely tolerated by society" and, to a certain extent, "permitted" by the government and judicial system, with the pertinent investigations not carried out or domestic violence cases shelved before being solved.

The authorities are similarly unconcerned—regardless of their political leanings—to raise awareness among the population about women's legal rights, procure the psychological treatment victims require, or to open the centres needed for them to find refuge.[55] According to data provided by Amnesty International, there should be one thousand four hundred women's shelters in Turkey, yet only thirty exist. Taking into account the country's total female population, this means that there is less than one refuge for every million women. Obviously, not enough. Even tougher is the fact that governments display a great deal of reticence when it comes to opening more centres.

If we journey beyond Istanbul, even in the suburbs of this great city, many women are still treated as a commodity and forced to marry men they find anything but attractive. This, at a very early age, a time when they should be studying. Virginity is their seal of quality and their sexual knowledge a grand manual based on false myths, where the sexual act is considered a male physiological need.

Their vagina will rip, it will hurt terribly, and it will not stop bleeding are ideas etched in the minds of these young women, who often finish up associating sex with a lack of control, violence, or abuse. This results in pathologies such as vaginismus, a sexual dysfunction where the vaginal muscles involuntarily spasm when any attempt at penetration is made. Terrible problems that, if treated, require long periods of therapy and are not always possible to overcome.[56] For those who dare to overstep the limits of decency and maintain sexual relationships before marriage, there is no alternative but hymen reconstruction, a practice that is frequent in modern-day Turkey.[57]

Honour crimes are another grave problem facing this still-patriarchal society. Many continue to view women's bodies as family property, which, in time, is transferred to the husband and finally to society as a whole.[58] Any questionable usage of this valued asset puts the good name of the whole family at risk. All except the woman, of course, as even honour itself is exclusive to men. Every year, over two hundred women fall victim to tradition, a deadly weapon.

In this real-life Turkey, stripped of its Orientalist hue, many women had no access to primary education until 1997, when schooling was made obligatory up to the age of eight. Now, thanks to concerted government campaigns, 98 percent of Turkish women have completed primary education. This figure takes a significant slide, however, if we refer to secondary education and even more so if we take into account the number of young women accessing university. Only 24 percent continue into higher education.[59]

Nor do many women achieve a professional career. Let us recall that only 24.9 percent manage to do so, that there are far greater numbers of men in management posts, and that women earn much lower salaries, 30 percent less than their male counterparts. Only 7 percent occupy board-level positions in private companies, according to data from the World Economic Forum.

Meanwhile, in parliament, only fifty out of five hundred elected members are female. In 1935, when Turkish women first stood for election, they won eighteen seats, which represented 4.6 percent of the total. Now, seventy-three years later, this figure has not even doubled. The obstacles have not disappeared. Women must have a very solid academic background in order to stand as candidates, although the same is not true of the opposite sex, for whom primary education is more than sufficient. A lack of financial independence, with much lower incomes than men, does not help when it comes to organising an electoral campaign. Nor does the patriarchal mentality, still unaddressed, meaning that women are either left off the electoral lists altogether or occupy the last posts, with little chance of being elected. The worst part, according to KADER, is that women who manage to gain a place in parliament do not dare to raise their voices and confront the gender issues so common in Turkey. In fact, very few have any track record in women's rights, most being lawyers or businesswomen loyal to their parties, which view them as presenting no threat to male well being. "They end up behaving like men," observe the Turkish NGOs.

However, as in the Ottoman harems, there are also stories of women who impose their authority, of Roxelanas. One prime minister, one president of the most important Turkish business association, another of the council of state and the last, the president of the constitutional court, as well as outstanding businesswomen who demonstrate every single day their will to succeed in a man's world. There are also feminists who struggle from NGOs to secure the rights of their oppressed fellow-countrywomen. KADER, Kadiger, Women for Women Human Rights, and Morçati are among the associations gaining greater visibility and influence both in society and within the corridors of power. An organisation exists to promote female cinema production and there are film festivals where women play a central role. Some journalists fight for women's liberation from their opinion columns and awareness-raising campaigns about domestic violence are becoming more frequent in newspapers and on the television. Writers who voice the demands, feelings and frustrations of their peers and a large number of women keen to change their situation. Progress has been made but there is still a long way to go and many problems to overcome.

Constant political instability does not aid Turkey's journey towards gender equality. The tense battle between moderate Islamists and secular nationalists places women—and their headscarves—at the very centre of political wrangling. If people really consider that this square of material is a symbol of a closed, backwards looking mind, then wouldn't university be the ideal place for women to enhance their knowledge and broaden their outlook? And if it is a political symbol, employed as part of a hidden Islamic agenda, must women be doubly discriminated, manipulated by men and also denied access to university, where they could enrich their knowledge and training? Because it seems that many of them are unwilling, or not allowed, to stop using the *türban*, which means that, in the end, their only option is to stay at home and take care of their children.

The main problem facing Turkish women does not stem from religion, from Islam, nor from the governments in power, but from the patriarchal tradition of this society whose sexism is so deep-rooted.

In any case, the current situation is a great improvement compared with that of the past. In the wake of negotiations for entrance to the European Union, a suitable legal framework has been created for gender equality. Now it only remains for this to be effectively implemented and not just on paper. The new Turkish civil and criminal code protects women like never before, placing them on an equal footing with men. Furthermore, female participation at the centres of power has grown over recent years, and there has been an increase in awareness of the problems concerning them. Among the key tasks assigned to Turkey if it wishes to form part of the EU club is to develop mechanisms that enable an effective improvement in the situation of women. Entrance to the Union would solve many of the problems facing them, but the idea that Turkey will finally achieve a seat in the European Parliament increasingly seems but an illusion.

Whatever occurs, with or without the help of the EU, Turkey should strive, once and for all, to rid itself of the patriarchal structure that subjugates women. Real gender equality must become an overriding priority not only for this and future governments but for the whole civil society of this vast nation. Let us leave the harems to Orientalist literature and the history books. This is the twenty-first century and Turkish women now, like never before, have a unique opportunity to achieve full liberation. Don't let it slip away.

References

PART ONE: THE UNWANTED

[1] Vildan Yirmibeşoğlu, *Toprağa Düşen Sevdalar* (2007).
[2] Nilufer Yilmaz, President of Kamer, in discussion with the author held in Diyarbakir during December 2008.
[3] We can stop these killings committed in the name of honour (KAMER Study, 2006).
[4] Nilufer Yilmaz in discussion with the author, President of KAMER held in Diyarbakir during December 2008.
[5] 2007 Honor Killings Report. Human Rights Presidency of Turkey. 25 June, 2008.
[6] Interview with Vildan Yirmibeşoğlu, writer, lawyer and President of the Human Rights Section at the Governor of Istanbul's Office. December 2008.
[7] Dan Bilefsky, How to avoid Honor Killings in Turkey? Honor suicide (New York Times, 16th July 2006).
[8] Personal interview with Vildan Yirmibeşoğlu, writer, lawyer and President of the Human Rights Section at the Governor of Istanbul's Office. December 2008.
[9] Information provided by the NGO, Women for Women Human Rights.

[10] Vildan Yirmibeşoğlu, Toprağa Düşen Sevdalar (2007).
[11] Vildan Yirmibeşoğlu, Toprağa Düşen Sevdalar (2007).
[12] Nilufer Yilmaz, President of KAMER in Diyarbakir, in discussion with the author December 2008.
[13] Pinar Ilkkaracan, Reforming the Penal Code in Turkey: The Campaign for the Reform of the Turkish Penal Code from a Gender Perspective, (Institute for Development Studies, 2007).
[14] Canan Arin, lawyer and founder of the women's NGOs, Morcati and KADER, in discussion with the author. December 2008
[15] Data provided by Amnesty International Turkey during an interview with the author in 2008.

PART 2: THE PIOUS

[16] Data provided by the NGO, AKDER.

PART 3: THE UNIMAGINABLE

[17] Turkish Statistics Institute. Population and Economics, 2006.
[18] Data provided by the Turkish Businesswomen's Association, Kagider.
[19] Data provided by the Turkish Businesswomen's Association, Kagider.
[20] World Economic Forum, Global Gender Gap Index, 2007. The Turkish Statistics Institute claims that 20.9% of women had paid work outside the agricultural sector in 2006.
[21] World Economic Forum, Global Gender Gap Index, 2007.
[22] Data provided by the NGO, KADER.
[23] Andrew Mango, Atatürk (Overlook, 2000).
[24] Islamic Calvanists, (Study carried out by the European Stability Initiative, 19th September 2005).
[25] Ildefonso González (Europa Press), El risotto se convierte en un plato estrella en Turquía tras una curiosa polémica ministerial (23rd July, 2007).
[26] Cosmopolitan, Turkish Edition. March, 2008.
[27] Women and Sexuality in Muslims Societies (Women For Women's Rights, New Ways, 2004).

[28] Ricardo Ginés, A vueltas con el tanga islamista (La Vanguardia, Diario de Istanbul, 15th September 2008).
[29] Dilek Cindoglu, Tests and Artificial Virginity in Modern Turkish Medicine. Women and Sexuality in Muslim Societies (Women For Women's Rights, New Ways, 2004).
[30] Ildefonso González (Europa Press), Demandan a un diario islamista por alargar con photoshop el minivestido de una modelo, (19th May, 2007).
[31] Sirin Tekeli (ed.), Women in Modern Turkish Society (1995).

PART 4: THE UNBELIEVERS

[32] Naim Güleryuz, The History of the Turkish Jews, (N. Güleryuz, Istanbul, 1991).
[33] María Antonia Bel Bravo, Raíces del Decreto de expulsión. Sefarad. Los judíos de España, (Sílex, 2001).
[34] María Antonia Bel Bravo, La Diáspora. Sefarad. Los judíos de España, (Sílex, 2001).
[35] Estimate provided during an interview with the author by Naim Güleyruz, Director of the Sephardic Museum in Istanbul and author of The History of Turkish Jews. There are no exact figures, with historians' estimates ranging from 90,000 to 400,000. Güleyruz considers that some 120,000 left Spain, with the majority – around 90,000 emigrating to the Ottoman Empire.
[36] Museum of Turkish Jews, Istanbul. The reference appears in Yossel Daath Number 40, Abraham Danom.
[37] Museum of Turkish Jews, Istanbul. The reference appears in the Nomology or Legal Discourses of Immanuel Aboad.
[38] María Antonia Bel Bravo, Sefarad. Los judíos de España, (Sílex, 2001).
[39] Pablo Martín Asuero, Estambul, el ejército otomano y los sefardíes en textos en español (Isis, Istanbul, 2003).
[40] Pablo Martín Asuero, Estambul, el ejército otomano y los sefardíes en textos en español (Isis, Istanbul, 2003).
[41] María Antonia Bel Bravo, Imperio Otomano. Sefarad. Los judíos de España (Sílex, 2001).
[42] Naim Güleryuz, The History of Turkish Jews (N. Güleryuz, Istanbul, 1991).

[43] Karen Gerson Sarhon, The Emancipation of Turkish-Sephardic Women: A Reflection on my own life.
[44] Karen Gerson, President of the Sephardic Women's Association in Istanbul, in discussion with the author.
[45] Karen Gerson Sarhon, The Image of Women in Judeo-Spanish Proverbs and Idioms.
[46] Estimate provided during an interview with the author by Naim Güleyruz, Director of the Sephardic Museum in Istanbul and author of The History of Turkish Jews.
[47] Francisco Veiga, El turco. Diez siglos a las puertas de Europa, (2006).
[48] Francisco Veiga, El turco. Diez siglos a las puertas de Europa, (2006).
[49] Interview by the author with Karen Gerson Sarhon, President of the Cultural Research Centre for Turkish Sephardic Women.
[50] Spanish Ministry of Justice.
[51] Danielle Rozenberg, El regreso de los judíos a España. Una minoría en el proceso democrático in Política y Sociedad, 12 (1993), Madrid.
[52] María Antonia Bel Bravo, Sefarad. Los judíos de España, (Sílex, 2001).

EPILOGUE

[53] Ilhan Akşit, The Mystery of the Ottoman Harem, (Akşit kültür ve Turizm Yayincilik, 2007).
[54] Burcu Turkay, Press Officer for Amnesty International, Turkey, in discussion with the author.
[55] Burcu Turkay, Press Officer for Amnesty International, Turkey, in discussion with the author
[56] Pinar Ilkkracan, President of Women for Women's Human Right, in a personal interview with the author.
[57] Women and Sexuality in Muslim Societies, (Women For Women's Rights, New Ways, 2004) and Dilek Cindoglu, Virginity Tests and Artificial Virginity in Modern Turkish Medicine.
[58] Canan Arin, lawyer and founder of the women's NGO, Morcati (Purple Ceiling).in a personal interview with the author.
[59] World Economic Forum, 2007. Global Gender Gap Index.

Printed in Dunstable, United Kingdom

66703499R00129